AGILE PROJECT MANAGEMENT

A PRACTICAL STEP–BY-STEP BEGINNER'S
GUIDE TO AGILE PROJECT MANAGEMENT
AND WORKABLE SOFTWARE
DEVELOPMENT

By Alex Turner

Table of Content

First published in 2019

Copyright © 2019 Alex Turner

INTRODUCTION

This book is intended to benefit project managers who are moving into project management. It will also be of curiosity to Agile developers who wish to know more about project management. And finally, it will also be of interest to anyone else who wants to know more about the management of agile projects. It is critical to note that agile is not a methodology but an approach that can utilize a variety of methodologies.

Agile uses organizational models based on people, collaboration, and values. The Agile Manifesto for the primary principles of the agile philosophy. It uses rolling wave planning, iterative and incremental delivery, rapid and flexible research to change, and open communication between teams, stakeholders, and customers the Agile Method is an approach to project management that is intended to help development teams effectively address the moving targets and uncertainties that identify the creation of new software applications. One of the hallmarks of Agile is that it uses an incremental, iterative series of work that is commonly known as "sprints."

A sprint is a time allocated for a specific phase of a development project, and it's considered to be complete when the period set for the phase expires. Work on that phase of the project ends, even if some team members think more effort is required. The next phase of the project begins and runs through its designated time frame, and so on until all the phases of the project are complete.

Many of the ideas behind Agile emerged in the 1970s as alternatives to traditional approaches to project development. But the term "Agile" in the context of software development was first popularized by the "Manifesto for Agile Software Development," created in 2001 by a set of experienced software developers who came to perceive that they were practicing software development differently from the classic waterfall methodology.

The manifesto documented their shared beliefs about how contemporary software development processes should operate, and the values and principles outlined in the manifesto were derived from and support a range of development models, such as Scrum and Kanban.

HISTORY OF AGILE

The frustrations of applying sequential project management methods to software development resulted in the emergence of Agile. A group of leading software developers met in Snowbird, Utah, the USA in 2001 to discuss their challenges. They ultimately created the Agile Manifesto.

What the software industry needed was greater agility– new methods that allowed for changes without significantly impacting cost and production schedules.

By dividing production into small components (called iterations) that could be and rapidly developed and tested, modifications could be made without having to wait for the end product.

Now agile methods are used in a variety of industries beyond software development, such as telecommunications, aerospace, and construction, as well as being blended with more traditional, linear project management approaches.

Agile is work a management methodology that can be implemented into most aspects of your business processes.

Originally conceived to be used in a software development context, agile emerged as a way to streamline operations back in the early 2000s when previous work management philosophies weren't cutting. Business leaders in the IT and software development space felt that tools conceived previously were clunky and slow and didn't allow the kind of responsiveness needed to shift plan of action as priorities change for different projects quickly.

Although agile is generally used in the IT and software development industry, it was initially devised as an alternative to Software Development Lifecycle methodologies and offers an iterative approach to software delivery.

Although agile was initially created to help businesses in an IT and software development context, the basic framework is applicable across every industry.

Agile dictates that software is built incrementally from the start of the project rather than attempting to deliver it all at the very end. Each project is broken down into smaller, bite-sized functions and is prioritized and given to different user types. Then those smaller mini-projects are continuously worked on and delivered over two-week spans called iterations.

While these are the basics of agile, the methodology follows a set of principles that dictate how businesses can become more streamlined via these guidelines. Here are a handful of ways to integrate this philosophy into your marketing plan.

THE AGILE PHILOSOPHY

The word 'philosophy' can be defined as a way of thinking about the world, the universe, and society. In effect, to 'be agile' involves adopting a new way of thinking or mindset that is based on agile values and principles.

This philosophy or mindset then guides your holistic approach to agile. The agile mindset needs to be internalized (e.g., welcoming change, delivering frequently), and it should steer the selection and implementation of agile practices. Being agile isn't about merely applying tools and techniques or following a methodology, applying agile philosophy and principles to how you use agile methods changes not only the approach but also the overall effectiveness (and success) of the practices.

As opposed to a traditional approach, Agile project management philosophy has been introduced as an attempt to make software engineering more flexible and efficient. With 94 percent of the organizations practicing agile in 2016, it has become the industry standard for project management.

The history of agile can be traced back to 1957: at that time, Bernie Dimsdale, John von Neumann, Herb Jacobs, and Gerald Weinberg were using incremental development techniques (which are now known as Agile), building software for IBM and Motorola. Although, not knowing how to classify the approach they were practicing, they realized clearly that it was different from Waterfall in many ways.

However, the modern-day agile approach was officially introduced in 2001, when a group of 17 software development professionals met to discuss alternative project management methodologies. Having a clear vision of the flexible, lightweight, and team-oriented software development approach, they mapped it out in the Manifesto for Agile Software Development.

Aimed at "uncovering better ways of developing software," the Manifesto specifies the fundamental principles of the new approach:

"Through this work, *we* have come to value:

- **Individuals and interactions** over processes and tools

- **Working software** over comprehensive documentation

- **Customer collaboration** over contract negotiation

- **Responding to change** over following a plan."

Complemented with the Twelve Principles of Agile Software, the philosophy has come to be a universal and efficient new way of managing projects.

Agile methodologies take an iterative approach to software development. Unlike a straightforward linear waterfall model, agile projects consist of several smaller cycles – sprints. Each one of them is a project in miniature: it has a backlog and consists of design, implementation, testing, and deployment stages within the pre-defined scope of work.

"Agile" software development is a rarity among business buzz words in that it is an apt description of what it seeks to accomplish. Optimally implemented, it is capable of delivering value and efficiency to business-IT partnerships by incorporating flexibility and an ability to pivot rapidly when necessary.

As a technology company with a longstanding management consulting pedigree, RiskSpan values the combination of discipline and flexibility inherent to Agile development and regularly makes use of the philosophy in executing client engagements. Dynamic economic environments contribute to business priorities that are seemingly in a near-constant state of flux. In response to these ever-evolving needs, clients seek to implement applications and application feature changes quickly and efficiently to realize business benefits early. This growing need for speed and "agility" makes Agile software development methods an increasingly appealing alternative to traditional "waterfall" methodologies. Waterfall approaches move in discrete phases—treating analysis, design, coding, and testing as an individual, stand-alone components of a software project.

Historically, when the cost of changing plans was high, such a discrete approach worked best. Nowadays, however, technological advances have made changing the plan more cost-feasible. In an environment where changes can be made inexpensively, rigid waterfall methodologies become unnecessarily counterproductive for at least four reasons:

When a project runs out of time (or money), individual critical phases—often testing—must be compressed, and overall project quality suffers.

Because working software isn't produced until the very end of the project, it is difficult to know whether the project is really on track before project completion.

Not knowing whether established deadlines will be met until relatively late in the game can lead to schedule risks.

Most important, discrete phase waterfalls do not respond well to the various ripple effects created by change.

Continuous Activities vs. Discrete Project Phases

Agile software development methodologies resolve these traditional shortcomings by applying techniques that focus on reducing overhead and time to delivery. Instead of treating fixed development stages as discrete phases, Agile treats them as *continuous activities*. Doing things simultaneously and continuously—for example, incorporating testing into the development process from day one—improves quality and visibility, while reducing risk. Visibility improves because being halfway through a project means that half of a project's features have been built and tested, rather than having many partially built features with no way of knowing how they will perform in testing. Risk is reduced because feedback comes in from the earliest stages of development and changes without paying exorbitant costs. This makes everybody happy.

Flexible but Controlled

Firms sometimes balk at Agile methods because of a tendency to equate "flexibility" and "agility" with a lack of organization and planning, weak governance and controls, and abandonment of formal documentation. This, however, is a misconception. "Agile" does not mean uncontrolled—on the contrary; it is no more or less controlled than the existing organizational boundaries of standardized processes into which it is integrated. Most Agile methods do not advocate any particular methodology for project management or quality control. Rather, their intent is on simplifying the software development *approach*, embracing changing business needs, and producing working software as quickly as possible. Thus, Agile frameworks are more like a shell in which users of the framework have full flexibility to customize as necessary.

Frameworks and Integrated Teams

Agile methodologies can be implemented using a variety of frameworks, including Scrum, Kanban, and XP. Scrum is the most popular of these and is characterized by producing a potentially shippable set of functionalities at the end of every iteration in two-week timeboxes called *sprints*. Delivering high-quality software after such short sprints requires supplementing team activities with additional best practices, such as automated testing, code cleanup, and other refactorings, continuous integration, and test-driven or behavior-driven development. Agile teams are built around motivated individuals subscribing to what is commonly referred to as a "lean Agile mindset." Team members who embrace this mindset share a common vision and are motivated to contribute in ways beyond their defined roles to attain success. In this way, innovation and creativity are supported and encouraged. Perhaps most important, Agile promotes building relationships based on trust among team members and with the end-user customer in providing fast and high-quality delivery of software. This is the aim of any worthwhile endeavor. When it comes to software development, Agile is showing itself to be an impressive means to this end.

Agile Development Cycle

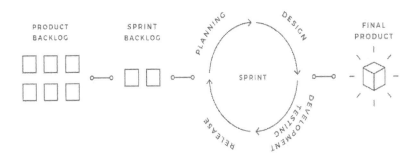

At the end of each sprint, a potentially shippable product increment is delivered. Thus, with every iteration, new features are added to the product, which results in gradual project growth. With the features being validated early in the development, the chances of delivering a potentially failed product are significantly lower. Let's summarize the main Agile aspects:

- **Flexibility:** The scope of work may change according to new requirements.

- **Work breakdown:** The project consists of small cycles (known as Sprints in Scrum).

- **Value of teamwork:** The team members work closely together and have a clear vision about their responsibilities.

- **Iterative improvements:** There is a frequent reassessment of the work done within a cycle to make the final product better.

- **Cooperation with a client:** A customer is closely engaged in the development and can change the requirements or accept the team's suggestions.

Prioritizing flexibility and rapid turnaround, the

The agile approach offers the following benefits,

according to recent research:

Ability to manage the changing priorities (88%)

Increased team productivity through daily task allocation (83%)

Better project visibility due to the simple planning system (83%)

Agile Frameworks

Agile is an umbrella term for a wide variety of methodologies and techniques, sharing the principles and values described above. Each of them has its areas of use and distinctive features. The most popular frameworks are Scrum, Kanban, Hybrid, Lean, Bimodal, and XP. Before discussing these frameworks in more detail, let's look at their key features.

Framework	Planned Mitigation
Scrum	• The entire scope of work is broken down into short development cycles — Sprints. • The Sprint's duration is from one to four weeks. • The team should strictly follow a work plan for each Sprint. • People involved in a project have predefined roles.
Kanban	• Development is built on workflow visualization. • The current work (work in progress or WIP) is prioritized. • There are no timeboxed development cycles. • The team can change the work plan at any time.
Hybrid	• Agile and Waterfall complement each other. • Agile software development is held under Waterfall conditions (fixed deadline, forecasted budget, and thorough risk assessment).
Bimodal	• There are two separate modes of work — traditional (Mode 1) and Agile (Mode 2). • Two separate teams are working on projects with two different goals. • The Mode 1 team maintains IT system infrastructure. • The Mode 2 team delivers innovative applications. • Cross-team collaboration is important
Lean	• The framework promotes fast software development with less effort, time, and cost. • The development cycle is as short as possible. • The product delivered early is being continuously improved. • The team is independent and has a wider range of responsibilities than those in Scrum, Bimodal, and Hybrid. • Developers can also formulate the product's concept
XP	• The focus is on technical aspects of software development. • XP introduces engineering practices aimed at helping developers write a clear code. • Product development includes consistent stages: core writing, testing, analyzing, designing, and continuous integration of code. • Face-to-face communication within the team and customer involvement in development are crucial

HOW AGILE ADDRESSES THE CAUSES OF DEVELOPMENT AND PROJECT FAILURES

Agile methodologies have been propounded increasingly for IS projects over the last ten years. Kent Beck introduced the concepts of extreme programming, (Agile XP), while in 1986 by Hirotaka Takeuchi and Ikujiro Nonaka in the "New Product Development Game" developed scrum. Both

evolved from a previous software development methodology: DSDM (Dynamic Systems Development Method). The DSDM Consortium are guardians of the agile project management framework surrounding all agile delivery methods.

The Agile Alliance has promoted joint application development methodologies with high user involvement in build decisions (Beck, 2000). These methods promote continuous monitoring and adapting of deliverables to meet fixed benefits. Unfortunately, due to the challenges of complexity, scale, and interconnectivity facing software engineers, the level of systems failure remains stubbornly high (e.g., Ewusi-Mensah & Przasnyski, 1994;

Doherty, & King, 2001). Indeed, a report by the British Computer Society [BCS, 2004] concluded that:

"Billions of pounds are wasted every year on new IT systems', as 'only around 16 percent of IT projects can be considered truly successful."

Laanti et al. (2011) examined an organization-wide adoption of agile practices at Nokia, and their results revealed that "respondents agreed with the benefits of agile usage, including higher satisfaction and effectiveness, increased quality and transparency, and earlier detection of faults and that 60% would prefer to stay with the methods than return to their previous ways of working."

Agile approaches emphasize business ownership of products and prioritize team efforts based on business benefits. The methodology aims to enhance team working and shared understanding of goals, based on a lean concept of "Voice of the Customer" and is akin to the lean six sigma process improvement approach.

All of these approaches advocate a key user who is empowered to prioritize the work of a self- sufficient team, with the project manager becoming a 'servant leader' who coaches the team for improvements, as well as addressing other disciplines such as wider stakeholder management to keep the team focused purely on delivery. The aim is to deliver earlier benefits by doing the highest value work first. However, the agile methodologies are less comprehensive, dealing predominantly with the software development stage. Some companies, such as Siemens, have adapted the tools and techniques and applied them to engineering work successfully, but their usage is still limited.

Most agile adoption has been driven from the software development arena, but there is a body of research now investigating whether other industries can use this methodology. Conforto (2014) states that "project planning and control is a challenge for companies engaged in developing new products and technologies" and that there is a drive to implement only pure agile project management. It is the aim of this study to investigate how often that occurs and whether partial adoption also brings benefits over a more traditional project approach.

THE BASICS AND ADVANTAGES OF AGILE PROJECT MANAGEMENT

Organizations who use agile principles and practices have documented the value they see from the philosophy and techniques:

•Adaptive to changing business needs, giving the organization more influence over adding, modifying, or removing requirements

•Early and continuous customer feedback improves communication and empowers business owners who can receive and review critical information necessary to make decisions to steer the project throughout the development process

•Early measurable return on investment

•High visibility and influence over the project progress leading to early indications of problems

•Incremental delivery rather than a single complete delivery at the end of the project; reduce product and process waste.

Analyzing the Key Business Benefits

The Agile method of software development presents several compelling potential benefits for companies. These benefits fall into two main categories: Company economic framework and people's perspectives.

Economic Framework

The Agile Method changes the way work is structured, and even the way organizations think about work. It introduces a shift in the way tasks are completed to increase productivity throughout the development lifecycle and at the same time boosting productivity.

The method is designed to create more efficient and productive ways of working that helps teams achieve better results and higher quality products that meet the needs of customers. The rise in efficiency comes because teams work in shorter cycles and are less likely to veer off in the wrong direction in terms of design and development.

Rather than working from development plans that are measured in months and even years, teams are expected to produce results within weeks. That means there is faster and regular feedback from customers, and many opportunities to make mid-course corrections to deliver what the customer wants at virtually every stage. By leveraging iterative planning and feedback, teams can continuously enhance products to reflect the needs of clients, and quickly adapt to changing requirements throughout the process by accurately measuring and evaluating project status at every stage.

Team members can learn during each cycle, and gain knowledge as they move along with a project. Because much of Agile is a collaborative process, this knowledge can be shared among colleagues as appropriate, building up the experience of the team as a whole.

The collaboration extends to the customers who will be using the software. Although customer needs can and do change over time, having continuous feedback during the development process dramatically reduces the likelihood of delivering products that are off the mark.

From a corporate results standpoint, all of this can lead to higher revenue from product sales, shorter time to market for new products and services, and increased the ability to compete.

Many might argue that in today's business environment, being agile in general is not a nice-to-have capability – it's a must-have. Customers expect companies to be highly agile, and if they're not, they will turn to competitors that meet this need.

PEOPLE'S PERSPECTIVE

It's a common sentiment that people are an organization's most valuable assets – and it's true.

Regardless of how much automation companies adopt as a result of advances in artificial intelligence, machine learning, robotics, and other areas, human workers are still the heart and soul of any business. They are the drivers of creativity and innovation.

"The Agile method can provide benefits from a people perspective because it can lead to happier employees and team. Better team collaboration fosters more cohesion and cooperation among developers."

When workers are satisfied, there is less likelihood of conflict among team members and less turnover, which means companies don't need to spend much of their time looking for new talent at a time when technology skills are challenging to come by.

When there is a need to expand development teams, fostering a positive work environment can make it easier to recruit people. The Agile Method can help provide a much better environment for innovation, the empowerment of teams, and the realization of creative potential. All these things are attractive to prospective employees.

The Agile Method can also lead to more satisfied customers. Because of the close collaboration between development teams and the ultimate users of the software, customers get a chance to share in the innovation and weigh in on what they think is essential. As a result, there is a much higher chance they will be pleased with the finished product.

HOW TO IMPLEMENT AGILE PROJECT MANAGEMENT INTO YOUR BUSINESS

Step 1: Set your vision with a strategy meeting

At the beginning of a new Agile project, you need to define a clear business need or insight that your project is addressing. In essence, you need to answer why you're doing what you're setting out to do? It's big-picture stuff, but this is the core belief that you'll refer back to as you build.

For product companies, one of the best ways to define your vision is to use what's called the **Elevator Pitch:**

For: (Our Target Customer)

Who: (Statement of the Need)

The: (Product Name) is a (Product Category)

That: (Key Product Benefit, Compelling Reason to Buy or Use)

Unlike: (Primary Competitive Alternative)

Our Product: (Final Statement of Primary Differentiation)

If you're not building a product, you can still probably see how you could quickly adjust this pitch to match your project's goals.

Who should be there?

This is where you get buy-in on your project, so as many vital stakeholders should be present, including relevant executives, managers, and directors, as well as all product owners.

When does it happen?

Your strategy meeting should happen before any project starts or at least annually to make sure your mission still is valid, with periodic meetings for updates.

This is subjective, but a proper strategy meeting can take anywhere from 4–16 hours (just not in a row!).

Step 2: Build out your product roadmap

Once your strategy has been validated, it's time for the product owner to translate that vision into a product roadmap. This is a high-level view of the requirements for your project with a loose timeframe for when you will develop each of them.

The 'loose' part here is essential. You're not spending days or weeks planning out every step, but merely identifying, prioritizing, and roughly estimating the effort each piece of your product will take on the way to making a usable product.

So, what does this look like for an Agile project? Product Management expert Roman Pichler suggests working with a goal-oriented product roadmap, which is sometimes also referred to as theme-based:

"Goal-oriented roadmaps focus on goals, objectives, and outcomes like acquiring customers, increasing engagement, and removing technical debt. Features still exist, but they are derived from the goals and should be used sparingly. Use no more than three to five features per goal, as a rule of thumb."

For each of these goals, you want to include five key pieces of information: Date, Name, Goal, Features, and Metrics.

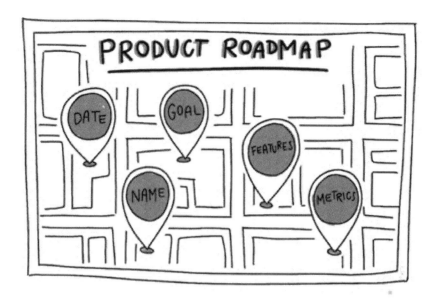

This gives you a clear idea of what needs to be done, when, and how you'll measure success.

Who should be there?

The product roadmap is done by the Product Owner, but should also include buy-in and input from any other stakeholders in the project—think marketing, sales, support, and development team reps.

When does it happen?

Like all things in Agile project management, you want to move rather than dwell on early-stage planning. However, your roadmap is a literal map from your mission to your MVP and should take as long as it does to feel confident that you've covered all the applicable goals.

Step 3: Get excited with a release plan

What is it?

Now that we've got a strategy and a plan, it's time to set some tentative timelines.

At this stage, the product owner creates a high-level timetable for the release of working software. Because Agile projects will have multiple versions, you'll want to prioritize the features needed to get you to launch first.

For example, if your project kicked off in November, you might set your MVP launch for early February, with a high-priority feature release the following May. This all depends on the complexity of your project and the lengths of your "sprints"—the periods of work dedicated to each goal (which we'll get into next!). A typical release includes 3–5 of these sprints.

Who should be there?

A release plan is like rallying the troops. The product owner, project managers, and all team members should be there. You can also bring in a few key stakeholders to add some additional oomph and get the team fired up.

At a minimum, your release plans should be created on the first day of any new release and reviewed at least every quarter.

How long should it take? Be realistic about how long a release will take, but don't let that slow you down. A typical release planning session should take around 4–8 hours.

Step 4: It's time to plan out your sprints

What is it?

It's time to move from the macro to the micro view as the product owner and development team plan "sprints"—short cycles of development in which specific tasks and goals will be carried out. A typical sprint lasts between 1–4 weeks and should remain the same length throughout the entire project as this enables teams to plan future work more accurately based on their past performance.

At the beginning of a sprint cycle, you and your team will create a list of backlog items you think you can complete in that timeframe that will allow you to develop functional software. Then, it's as simple as using one of the Agile methodologies to work through them (which we'll cover more in-depth below).

Who should be there?

Sprint planning is a team effort, and therefore the product owner, project managers, and all team members should be present to voice their thoughts and concerns.

When does it happen?

Sprint planning takes place at the start of each sprint cycle. For example, if you're making weekly sprints, you'll do a planning session every Monday (or whatever day of the week you choose to start on).

How long should it take?

Sprint planning sets the tone for the cycle. So while you don't want to spend too much time at this stage, it could realistically take you 2–4 hours. But once you've planned your sprint, you're quite literally off to the races.

Step 5: Keep your team on track with daily stand-ups

Throughout every sprint, you need opportunities to make sure no roadblocks are creeping up and getting in the way of completing your goals on time. That's where the daily meeting, or "Standup" in Agile-speak, comes in.

A standup is a daily, 15-minute meeting where your team comes together to discuss three things:

What did you complete yesterday?

What are you working on today?

Are there any roadblocks getting in the way?

While this might seem like an annoyance to some of your team, these meetings are essential for fostering the kind of communication that drives Agile project management. Agile depends on reacting quickly to issues, and voicing them in a public space is a powerful way to foster cross-team collaboration.

Step 6: Sprint's made? It's time for a review

What is it?

If everything has gone as planned, by the end of your sprint cycle, you should have a functioning piece of software. At this point, it's time to review what was done and show this off to people on your team and any key stakeholders. Think of it as Agile show-and-tell.

The key here is to check your initial plan to make sure that all requirements were met. As the product owner, it's your choice to accept or refuse certain functionalities. If something went wrong, ask why? How can you adjust the next sprint so your team can hit their targets? Agile is all about continuous learning and iterations, and this means on your processes as well as your product.

Who should be there?

Your entire team, as well as any key stakeholders, should be at your sprint review to check in on progress and voice their support.

When does it happen?

The sprint review takes place at the end of each sprint

How long should it take?

Just say no to PowerPoint's and feature dissertations. The sprint review should only take an hour or two max.

Step 7: What's next? Decide what to focus on in your sprint retrospective

What is it?

For Agile project management to work, you need to have a clear next step after each step. This is determined during your sprint retrospective. Once a sprint has been completed, and features have been shown off, it's time to decide what work gets done next. Did you learn something during the sprint that changes your initial timeline or vision for the project?

Don't merely plan, but also take this time to discuss how the previous sprint went and how you could improve in your next one.

Who should be there?

The retrospective is a natural extension of the review, and so while your stakeholders can leave, the rest of the team should be involved and giving their insights

When does it happen?

It makes the most sense for your sprint retrospective to happen right after your sprint review.

How long should it take?

Again, keep it short and sweet. An hour or two max is probably all you'll need to debrief and plan for the next brief.

What happens now?

At this point, you should have a functional piece of software you can ship, get feedback on, and plan new features or fixes. This continuous shipping, learning, and building are what makes Agile so powerful. Rather than directly working through your backlog, you're releasing products and seeing how people interact with them. This means rather than work on a product for a year only to release it and find out some core functionality is missing, and you could potentially figure that out after a sprint and adjust accordingly.

HOW TO APPLY THE AGILE PROJECT MANAGEMENT METHOD EFFECTIVELY

The top three Agile methodologies explained

At this point, you might feel ready to dive into Agile and bring it to your team. However, there's one more step we need to go through. As we said earlier, Agile is more of a blanket term for a philosophy of project management and development. To use these ideas to their fullest, some brilliant people have developed Agile methodologies you can follow.

These methodologies are all quite similar, but from an implementation standpoint, each has its mix of practices, terminology, and tactics.

Let's take a look at the top 3 and break down how they're different: Scrum is probably the most well-known Agile methodology, and often the two go hand-in-hand. It's especially popular in the software development world thanks to its simplicity, proven productivity, and ability to act as a catch-all framework for the various practices promoted by other Agile methodologies.

<u>Here's how it works</u>:

With Scrum, the "Product Owner" works closely with their team to identify and prioritize their goals or features and add these to what's called a "Product Backlog." The backlog can consist of features, bug fixes, non-functional requirements—pretty much anything that needs to be done to deliver working software.

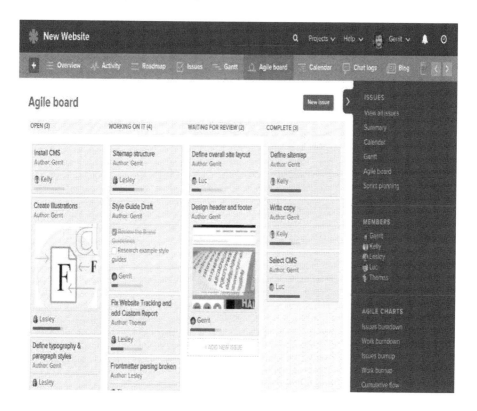

With this backlog in place, the Product Owner decides priorities and teams sign up to deliver "potentially shippable increments" of software during their Sprints, which typically last 30 days. Once the team has committed to that Sprint's backlog, nothing else can be added to it except by the organization. At the end of that 30-day Sprint, the backlog is analyzed and reprioritized (if necessary), and the whole thing starts over.

Like Scrum, Kanban is an Agile methodology built around continual delivery, while keeping things simple and not overburdening the development team. Kanban is based around three basic principles:

Visualize your workflow on a "board"

Being able to see all the items you're working on in the context of each other can be incredibly informative and help keep things clear and straightforward when projects get complex. Kanban tools (like Planio!) use a 'board' style to see all your items and where they fit in the flow from to-do to doing to do.

Keep your work-in-progress (WIP) limited

Have clear next steps

Extreme Programming (XP)

Extreme Programming (XP) isn't absolute in the Mountain Dew sense, but it is a bit of a departure from the other methodologies we've discussed.

XP is a more disciplined approach to Agile project management that involves high customer involvement, rapid feedback loops, continuous testing and planning, and close teamwork to deliver working software quickly. To give you an idea, a typical XP Sprint lasts only 1–3 weeks.

The original XP 'recipe' described by software engineer Kent Beck, was based around four values—simplicity, communication, feedback, and courage—with 12 supporting practices. It's more complicated than other methodologies and looks something like this in practice:

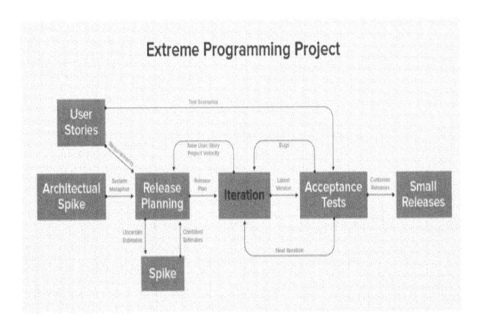

In XP, there are tight feedback loops where the "customer" works closely with the team to define and prioritize granular goals called "User Stories." The team then estimates, prioritizes, and plans the delivery of these stories, getting more feedback from the customer until it's ready for release.

Final thoughts on implementing Agile project management

Congratulations! It would help if you now had a clear understanding of what Agile project management looks like and a few of the compelling ways you can use it on your teams.

However, there is one last piece of the puzzle. With all of this information, organization, and prioritization happening, you need a proper project management tool to keep your Agile project on course. The best software addresses three pain points common to the Agile project management process:

Reporting and Metrics: Things like time tracking and projection, easy-to-understand progress reports for stakeholders, quality assurance, and a big-picture look at the progress

Communication: The ability to keep everyone on track with updates to local and distributed teams, shared task lists, feedback, and assignments.

<u>Project assessment</u>: Functionality around identifying and remedying obstacles or bottlenecks, evaluating performance, and making sure financials are under control.

THE MAIN BENEFITS OF APPLYING THE AGILE METHOD

- Agile project teams achieve faster time-to-market and consequentially cost savings. They start development earlier than in traditional approaches because agile approaches minimize the exhaustive upfront planning and documentation that is conventionally part of the early stages of a waterfall project.

- Agile development teams are self-organizing and self-managing. The managerial effort usually put into telling developers how to do their work can be applied to removing impediments and organizational distractions that slow down the development team.

- Agile development teams determine how much work they can accomplish in an iteration and commit to achieving those goals. Ownership is fundamentally different because the development team is establishing the commitment, not complying with an externally developed obligation.

- An agile approach asks, "What is the minimum we can do to achieve the goal?" instead of focusing on including all the features and extra refinements that could be needed. An agile approach usually means streamlining: barely sufficient documentation, removal of unnecessary meetings, avoidance of inefficient communication (such as email), and less coding (just enough to make it work).

- By encapsulating development into short sprints that last one to four weeks or less, you can adhere to the goals of the current iteration while accommodating a change in subsequent iterations. The period of sprint remains the same throughout the project to provide a predictable rhythm of development for the team long-term.

- Planning, elaborating on requirements, developing, testing, and demonstrating functionality occur within an iteration, lowering the risk of heading in the wrong direction for extended periods or promoting something that the customer doesn't want.

- Agile practices inspire a steady pace of development that is productive and healthy. For example, in the popular Agile development set of practices called extreme programming (XP), the maximum workweek is 40 hours, and the preferred workweek is 35 hours. Agile projects are sustainable and more productive, especially long term.

Check out the presentation on the adverse effects of **"Racing in Reverse."**

- Priorities, experience on the existing project, and, eventually, the speed at which development will likely happen within each sprint is precise, making for the right decisions about how much can or should be achieved in a period.

If you've ever worked on a project before, you might have a basic understanding of project management activities.

HOW THE AGILE METHOD CAN COMPARE TO THE WATERFALL METHOD AND OTHER TRADITIONAL PROJECT MANAGEMENT METHODS

The **waterfall method** is a traditional project management approach that uses sequential phases to define, build, test, and release project deliverables. Each level is completed and approved before the team moves on to the next stage. The project can't move back to previous phases.

Agile is an umbrella term covering several newer project management approaches that use iterative work cycles, called sprints. Each sprint uses 'mini-phases' to define, build, test, and release the project deliverables.

You show the audience a visual comparing the two methods, which shows how the waterfall method is a sequential process while agile methods are iterative cycles from the beginning to the end of the project.

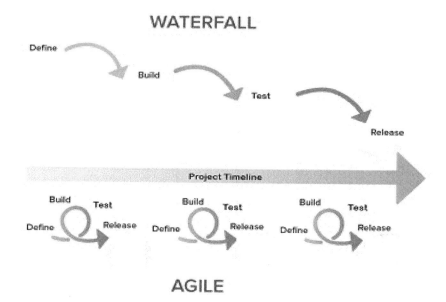

What Are the Differences?

It looks like your audience gets the different methods, but diving deeper will be helpful. The main difference between waterfall and agile methods is in the goals; the waterfall method wants to get everything right the first time, and agile methods wish to get things freed quickly. The difference in adaptability, documentation, testing, and collaboration supports different goals. Let's look at each a little closer.

Bimodal: traditional Waterfall combined with Agile

The Bimodal approach is quite popular: It is estimated that 16 percent of companies choose it. Gartner introduced the term "Bimodal IT" in 2014. Bimodal is the practice of managing two separate but consistent styles of work: one focused on predictability and the other on agility.

Mode 1 is traditional; thus, it works perfectly in well-understood and predictable areas. According to Gartner, it focuses on exploiting what is known while transforming the legacy environment into a state fit for a digital world.

Mode 2 involves rapid application development. It is exploratory, nonlinear, and optimized for solving new problems. Mode 2 is especially useful for working on projects that need to be finished as quickly as possible.

Both modes require different skills, techniques, and tools. Therefore, two separate workgroups are needed. These teams have two distinct goals — ensuring stability while adopting innovations. Team members focus on projects that suit their mode best.

The Mode 1 team develops and maintains applications and core systems to support long-term business needs. A company's technological capabilities depend directly on the work that's done by this team.

The Mode 2 team frequently delivers innovative applications to engage new customers and meet short-term business needs. This team may change the product's functionality after having received feedback and analyzed the market.

The teams use different delivery mechanisms and report them through different organizational structures. Nevertheless, they need to communicate with each other to exchange ideas and share results.

As Sandy Kemsley specifies, Mode 2 relies on the information and services infrastructure provided by Mode 1, while Mode 1 relies on Mode 2 for testing both new product ideas and new development methods that may eventually be rolled back into Mode 1.

When to use Bimodal

If the company specializes in both long- and short-term projects that require different development and management approaches, Bimodal might be the right choice. This framework is about keeping the balance between maintaining IT system infrastructure and driving innovations. When successfully implemented, Bimodal helps organizations quickly deliver solutions that users need to stay competitive.

Lean: Eliminating Waste in Software Engineering

According to the latest estimates, 17 percent of organizations adopt **Lean**. Its popularity decreased from 2015 to 2016. Nevertheless, this framework remains one of the 5 most widely used Agile frameworks. Having the same origins as Kanban, the approach started as a technique applied to physical manufacturing. It stemmed from Toyota Production System as a management approach aimed at *"making the vehicles ordered by customers in the quickest and most efficient way, in order to deliver the vehicles as quickly as possible."*

The application of Lean principles to software development was initially introduced by Mary and Tom Poppendieck in their book Lean Software Development: An Agile Toolkit.

It includes seven basic principles:

- Eliminate waste
- Amplify learning and create knowledge
- Decide as late as possible
- Deliver as fast as possible
- Empower the team
- Build integrity/quality in
- See the whole

Now let's have a closer look at these principles.

- **It is eliminating waste.** In terms of a project, the term "waste" refers to anything that is not adding value to the project and thus should be eliminated. In software engineering, this can be idle time, unnecessary features, or defects.

- **Amplify learning and create knowledge.** In Lean, software development is perceived as an ongoing learning process. Developers don't usually write clear code on the first try. After having detected and fixed errors, they write an improved variation of the previous code. Engineers gain knowledge during development by solving problems and producing code variations. So, the best way to improve the software development environment is to amplify learning.

+ **Decide as late as possible**. Late decisions are more informed ones because they are based on facts. Keeping in mind that technologies become obsolete increasingly faster, delaying an irreversible design decision is a wise move. A major strategy for making commitments late is to reserve the capacity for the change in the system.

+ **Deliver as fast as possible**. The fourth principle is about the pros of fast software development. Short development cycles allow developers to learn more by getting feedback. They also allow a customer to delay making a final decision about design until they know more. So, fast delivery helps eliminate waste.

+ **Empower the team.** Developers should have the right to make technical decisions as they understand the details of their work like no one else. They can create a roadmap and follow it.

- **Build-in integrity/quality.** The user's perception of the software and its characteristics must coincide. If a customer thinks that software has all the needed features and is easy to use, that system has perceived integrity. Conceptual integrity means that the software has a coherent architecture, and scores high on usability and fitness of purpose. It can be maintained, adapted, and extended.

- **See the whole.** Engineers should take charge of the overall efficiency of the system, instead of focusing on their small portion. If experts adhere to this principle, they can create a system with integrity.

These fundamentals perfectly describe Lean philosophy: it aims to deliver more value through less effort, investment, and time.

Lean software development is an **Iterative and Incremental Framework.** Therefore, as in any other

Agile approach, the working product increment is delivered at the early stages of development. Further progress depends mainly on the product owner's feedback.

What differentiates the Lean approach is that the team is not restricted from using any formal processes, such as recurring meetings or thorough task prioritization.

When to Use Lean

Lean allows companies to follow a minimum viable product (MVP) development technique. It includes a deployment of a product with a minimum, sufficient set of features to satisfy early users. The idea of the MVP strategy is to gather and analyze customer feedback to know if they like this product and want to buy it. Knowledge of customers' habits, tastes, and needs is the key to producing commercially successful products. Developers use feedback to create a roadmap for future development.

Lean works well for small, short-term projects due to their short life cycles. This approach is also appropriate if the customer can participate in a project realization as Lean requires ongoing feedback. Another important condition for the adoption of Lean is that the whole team should work in one office to enable communication.

Being effectively adopted by a vast number of manufacturing companies, like Nike, Ford, and Intel, Lean principles are widely used in other industries. Startups and successful companies, e.g., Corbis, PatientKeeper, and Xerox, apply Lean software engineering practices to their processes.

Extreme Programming: Engineering Practices For Writing A Good Code

Extreme Programming (XP) differs from the frameworks mentioned above by its focus on the technical aspects of software development. XP is used at 9 percent of companies.

It combines the most essential, providing agile teams with many tools to optimize the engineering process. Extreme Programming is a set of certain practices, applied to software engineering to improve its quality and ability to adapt to the changing requirements.

XP requires developers to perform a little number of engineering practices on the highest, almost extreme level possible, hence the name.

XP was introduced in the 1990s. Kent Beck, one of the initial signatories of the Agile Manifesto, invented it while working on a Chrysler Comprehensive Compensation System project. He aimed at finding ways of doing sophisticated tasks as expeditiously as possible. In 1999, he documented XP practices in the book Extreme Programming Explained: Embrace Change. The most commonly used XP practices are:

Test-Driven Development (TDD)

Refactoring

Continuous Integration

Pair Programming

Test-Driven Development is an advanced engineering technique that uses automated unit tests to propel the software design process. As opposed to the regular development cycle, where the tests are written after the code (or not written at all), TDD has a test-first approach. This means that the unit tests are written before the code itself.

According to this approach, the test should fail first when there is no code to accomplish the function. After that, the engineers write the code, focusing on the functionality to make the test pass. As soon as it's done, the source code should be improved to pass all the tests. These three steps are often referred to as the RedGreen-Refactor cycle.

TDD has proven to provide the following **benefits:**

- The tests are used to capture any defects or mistakes in the code, providing constant feedback on the state of every software component. Thus, the quality of the final product is increasingly high.
- The unit tests can be used as an always up-to-date project documentation, changing as the project evolves.

- Being deeply involved in product development, the team needs to be able to critically analyze it and foresee the planned outcome to test it properly. This keeps the team motivated and engaged, contributing to product quality.
- With thorough initial testing, the debugging time is minimized.
- Apart from being used within the TDD cycle, **Code refactoring** is a common practice in agile software development. It's a process of constant code improvement through simplification and clarification. The process is solely technical and does not call for any changes in software behavior.

- Extending the source code with each iteration, agile teams use refactoring as a way to weed out code clutter and duplications. This helps prevent software rot, keeping the code easy to maintain and extend.

Continuous Integration (CI) is another agile practice teams rely on for managing shared code and software testing. We believe CI is an evolutionary development of the Agile principles. Instead of doing short iterations, developers can commit newly written parts of code several times a day. This way, they constantly deliver value to users.

To verify the quality of the software — through testing — and automate its deployment, teams usually use Tools like CruiseControl, Atlassian Bamboo, TeamCity, or Jenkins.

Also, CI helps maintain the shared code, eliminating the integration issues. Thus, the product's mainline is robust and clean and can be rapidly deployed.

Pair Programming, or "pairing," is considered to be a very controversial agile practice. This technique requires two engineers working together. While one of them is writing the code, the other one is actively involved as a watcher, making suggestions and navigating them through the process.

Being focused on both code and more abstract technical tasks, this team of two is expected to be more efficient, creating better software design and making fewer mistakes. Another benefit of this approach lies in spreading the project knowledge across team members.

However, this practice has often been accused of harming the team's short-term productivity. The research shows that each task usually requires 15-60 percent more time, which is a major drawback of the approach. Yet, there are some opinions that the extra time is easily compensated in the long term through the overall higher quality of the software.

When to Use XP

XP provides tools to decrease risks while developing a new system, especially when developers must write code within strict timeframes. It's essential to know that XP practices are designed for small teams that don't exceed 12 people. One should choose this framework if sure that not only developers but also customers and managers will be able to work together on a project.

XP suggests unit testing, as well. If programmers have enough experience creating functional tests, then XP can be used.

Extreme Programming offers engineering practices and ideas that help development teams adapt to ever-changing requirements. The key features of this framework are a high rate of customer engagement and short iterative cycles that don't exceed one week. Also, XP suggests that developers make the simplest design possible and prioritize tasks.

While XP can be used as an independent framework, some of its technical practices have become a part of other Agile approaches. Ten percent of companies choose the Scrum/XP Hybrid framework, where XP engineering practices coexist with Scrum management approaches. For instance, Hybrid includes Scrum events and artifacts. The customer role evolves: it defines a Product Backlog and works together with a Development Team in the office until the project ends.

WHAT IS SCRUM

Scrum's origins can be traced back to an article that appeared in the January 1986 Harvard Business Review, entitled "The New Product Development Game."

It contrasts Waterfall-like practices at the National Aeronautics and Space Administration (NASA) to novel approaches at companies like 3M, Fuji-Xerox, Honda, and Cannon.

The Waterfall approach is likened to a relay-race, while strategies at successful companies were portrayed as being more akin to rugby teams '' moving the scrum downfield" (Takeuchi and Nonaka 1984). Over time, what called the "Rugby Approach" later morphed into Scrum.

Scrum is an iterative, incremental framework for projects and products or application development. Scrum is the most popular approach to implement agile. It helps to manage software development with an iterative approach. There are fixed-length iterations known as a sprint that allows shipping software frequently. It structures development in cycles of work called Sprints (Deemer et al. 2009). A race lasts one to two weeks, and at the end of each sprint, the stakeholders and team members conduct a meeting to prioritize and select a subset of the features of the software to implement.

At the end of each sprint, completed features are demonstrated to the customer or user, whose feedback is incorporated into the software in later sprints. This methodology also calls for short daily stand-up meetings, also known as daily scrums, where team members exchange information on progress, next tasks, and surface issues and roadblocks so that they are dealt with quickly. Each sprint culminates with a set of completed software features that are "potentially shippable above is simplified.

The roles, responsibilities, and meetings are fixed in a Scrum. In each sprint, there is sprint planning, daily stand-up, sprint demo, and sprint retrospective. There are task boards and burndown charts to follow up on the progress of the sprint as well as to receive incremental feedback.

Scrum: Roles, Sprints, and Artifacts

Scrum is a dominant agile methodology. It's used exclusively by 58 percent of organizations, while another 18 percent of the companies combine it with other techniques. First described in 1986 by Hirotaka Takeuchi and Ikujiro Nonaka in the New Product Development Game, it was formulated almost a decade after. In 1995, Ken Schwaber and Jeff Sutherland, the authors of the Scrum Guide, presented it at the OOPSLA conference. The presentation was based on the knowledge they acquired as they applied the method during the previous few years. While Scrum was introduced far before the Agile Manifesto, it relies on Agile principles and is consistent with the values stated in that document.

Scrum is aimed at sustaining active collaboration between people working on complex products, and details are being changed or added. It is based upon the systematic interactions between the three major roles: Scrum Master, Product Owner, and the Team.

Sprints and Artifacts

A basic unit of work in the scrum – **sprint** – is a short development cycle that is needed to produce a shippable product increment. A sprint usually is between 1 and 4 weeks long: More lengthy iterations lack the predictability and flexibility that are scrum's fundamental benefits. Having no standard duration (as long as it is less than four weeks), all the sprints within a project should have a fixed length. This makes it easier to plan and track progress.

ROLES IN A SCRUM:

Product Owner

The Product Owner communicates the vision for the software to be built. Product Owner not only focuses on the work to be completed but also focuses on business and market requirements. The PO interacts with the team as well as other stakeholders to build and manage the backlog. The role of a PO is to motivate the team to align them with the goal and vision of the project.

Scrum Master

Scrum Master is responsible for organizing meetings, dealing with challenges, and bottlenecks. The Scrum Master interacts with the Product Owner to ensure that the product backlog is ready for the next sprint. He or she is also responsible for ensuring that the group follows the Scrum process.

Scrum Team

The Scrum Team can be comprised of 5 to 7 members. In a Scrum team, there are no distinct roles as a programmer, designer, or tester; rather, everyone has a set of tasks that they complete together.

A basic unit of work in the scrum – **sprint** – is a short development cycle that is needed to produce a shippable product increment. A sprint usually is between 1 and 4 weeks long: More lengthy iterations lack the predictability and flexibility that are scrum's fundamental benefits. Having no standard duration (as long as it is less than four weeks), all the sprints within a project should have a fixed length. This makes it easier to plan and track progress.

Steps in the Scrum flow:

Scrum relies on **three main artifacts** that are used to manage the requirements and track progress – Product backlog, Sprint backlog, Sprint burndown chart. The process is formalized through several recurring meetings, like Daily Scrum (Standup), Sprint Planning, Review, and Retrospective meetings.

Product backlog

The product backlog comprises a list of all the desired features of the product. The Product Owner and Scrum Master prioritize the items based on user stories and requirements. The development team refers to the product backlog to complete the task during each sprint.

Sprint planning

In the sprint planning meeting, the Product Owner provides a list of high priority items on the backlog. The team chooses the task they can complete during the sprint and transfer the tasks from the product backlog to the sprint backlog.

Backlog refinement

The team and Product Owner meet at the end of each sprint to prepare the backlog for the next sprint. The team splits the user stories into a smaller chunk of tasks and removes any irrelevant user stories. The team also accesses the priority of stories to reprioritize tasks.

Daily Scrum

A 15-minute stand-up meeting known as Daily Scrum is conducted daily. The team member discusses the goals and issues related to development. The Daily Scrum is held every day during the sprint to keep the team on track.

SCRUM MEETINGS

This meeting is held to reflect on the success of the Scrum process and is there any changes required to be made in the next sprint. The team discusses the highs and lows of the earlier sprint and all the improvements for the next sprint.

The process is formalized through several recurring meetings, like the Daily Scrum (Standup), the Sprint Planning, the Review, and Retrospective meetings (the Sprint Retrospective).

The **Daily Scrum** is a time-boxed meeting, during which a Development Team coordinates its work and sets a plan for the next 24 hours. The event lasts 15 minutes and should be held daily at the same place and time.

The work to be completed is planned at the **Sprint Planning**. Everyone involved in the Sprint (a Product Owner, a Scrum Master, and a Development Team) participates in this event. They answer two key questions: which work can be done and how this work will be done. The Sprint Planning lasts no longer than eight hours for a one-month Sprint. For shorter Sprints, the meeting usually takes less time.

At the end of each sprint, the team and the product owner meet at the **Sprint Review**. During this informal meeting, the team shows the work completed and answers questions about the product increment. All participants collaborate on what to do next to increase the product's value. The Sprint Review is a four-hour time-boxed meeting for one-month Sprints.

The whole team goes to **Retrospective Meetings** to reflect on their work during the Sprint. Participants discuss what went well or wrong, find ways to improve, and plan how to implement these positive changes. The Sprint Retrospective is held after the Review and before the next Sprint Planning. The event's duration is three hours for one-month Sprints.

When to Use Scrum

Scrum works well for long-term, complex projects that require stakeholder feedback, which may greatly affect project requirements. So, when the exact amount of work can't be estimated, and the release date is not fixed, Scrum may be the best choice.

By setting customer needs and on-time/on-budget delivery as the highest priority, Scrum has gained the trust of 89 percent of Agile users. Thus, the list of companies using this approach is impressive. There is a public spreadsheet with such organizations, including Microsoft, IBM, Yahoo, and Google.

The latest research by the Scrum Alliance suggests that Scrum goes beyond IT. Companies working in the fields of finance, consulting, education, retail, media, and entertainment choose this approach to organize their work processes and enhance cooperation with customers. In 2016, the majority of the State of Scrum Report respondents (98 percent) said they are going to use this framework to move forward.

Kanban: Comprehensive Solution to Handling Work in Progress

Another joint project management framework is **Kanban**. Forty-three percent of companies have stated that they use Kanban as one of the project management frameworks. Originating from a visual system of cards used in Toyota manufacturing as a production control method, Kanban is simple, yet the powerful, approach to developing software products.

Kanban Board

BACKLOG

IN PROGRESS

COMPLETED

Translated as the visual signal from Japanese, Kanban focuses on the visualization of the workflow and prioritizes the **work in progress (WIP)**, limiting its scope to match it effectively to the team's capacity. As soon as a task is completed, the team can take the next item from the pipeline. Thus, the development process offers more flexibility in planning, faster turnaround, clear objectives, and transparency.

No standard procedures within the process, as well as the fixed iterations, are required in Kanban, as opposed to Scrum. The project development is based on the workflow visualization through a **Kanban board**, usually represented by sticky notes and whiteboards or online tools like Trello.

Trello automates and digitalizes Kanban. Due to the succinct information about a work item each Kanban card contains, everyone in the team knows who is responsible for the item, what each person's task is, when it's supposed to be finished, etc. Team members can also leave comments, attach screenshots, documents, or links to provide more details.

Teams using Kanban tools work cooperatively. The ability to track progress helps coworkers understand everyone's input in achieving the common goal, resulting in a focus on completing the task well and on time.

When to Use Kanban

Using Kanban, teams can do small releases and adapt to changing priorities. Unlike Scrum, there are no sprints with their predefined goals. Kanban is focused on doing small pieces of work as they come up. For example, if testers find errors in the product, developers try to fix them right away. Kanban, for instance, works well after the main release of the product.

Companies like Spotify and Wooga (leading mobile games development company) have been using this approach successfully over the years. Yet, 8 percent of organizations combine Scrum with Kanban techniques, using so-called **Scrumban** rather than the original frameworks.

Hybrid: Blend of Waterfall and Agile (Flexible Development and Thorough Project Planning)

Agile and Waterfall are two different visions of software development management. The former is about iterative development and being flexible, while the latter, promoting step-by-step development, requires careful planning, and rejects making changes along the way.

Twenty-three percent of companies realized that using principles of both approaches can be more beneficial than choosing one of the two. The combination of the traditional Waterfall project management approach and Agile is called Hybrid.

Specialists use the advantages of the Agile philosophy for software development. When it comes to budgeting, planning, and hardware set up, Waterfall works well. On the other hand, by embedding Agile practices into a traditional Waterfall work process, companies can increase the chances of realizing successful projects. For example, project planning can be done in sprints, testing can be incorporated in development, and feedback can be gathered regularly. Other ways of modifying the

Waterfall model include using Kanban boards and organizing retrospectives.

It should be noted that the choice of a hybrid framework's features may depend on the project. The hybrid frameworks not only imply using both approaches, depending on the project phase but also include options to inject Agile practices into a Waterfall process.

When to use Hybrid

Hybrid is an effective solution when product delivery relies on both hardware and software operations. But, there is another reason to choose Hybrid. The situation in which a customer is not satisfied with an unspecified timeframe and budget, as well as the lack of planning, is not rare. Such uncertainty is typical for Agile. In this case, planning, requirements specification, and application design can be accomplished in Waterfall. Agile is in place for software development and testing.

HOW SCUM RELATES TO AGILE

Agile is the software development methodology that focuses on customer satisfaction by delivering shippable software frequently. Scrum is one of the many approaches to implement Agile. Scrum is suitable for certain types of projects where there are rapidly changing requirements.

RECENT EXPERIENCE WITH SCRUM

In 2010, a new opportunity to employ agile development presented itself: the FAA was seeking to upgrade it is terminal ATC systems' data recording capabilities. The deployed systems were recording data on outdated storage media. Accurately, data was recorded onto magnetic tapes using DAT (Digital Archive Tape) drives, and the FAA wanted to upgrade the system and software to perform data recording onto RAID (Redundant Array of Independent Disks) storage devices, for many appropriate reasons such as reliability, redundancy, capacity, and performance. The effort was dubbed "CDR-R" for Continuous Data Recorder Replacement. The software changes required to make this transition were complex and non-trivial, requiring modifications to portions of the baseline code, some of which dated back to the 80s. Data recording is a critical component of the system – the FAA takes it very seriously, as they should, since this data is used not just for incident investigation purposes, but also to support data analysis of FAA operations.

The problem was that the scope of the changes that we estimated would be needed to implement the solution was such that they did not fit into the customer's yearly budget and schedule. This seemed to me to be an opportunity to try a new delivery approach: First, inspired by Feature Driven Design (FDD,) I proposed that we divide the scope of changes into a set of 'features' such as 'RAID recording', 'RAID synchronization', 'data transfer', etc. Then, inspired by the spiral development model, I proposed an incremental delivery of the CDR-R changes in three phases: the first phase would provide necessary RAID-based recording capabilities, the second would add additional monitoring and control capabilities for the RAIDs and provide data transfer tools to allow migration of data across various media and system installations, and finally the third phase would add some data maintenance functions. This new (in our program's context) delivery model made the CDR-R transition more palatable for our customers and made for a better fit with their funding cycles, leading them to authorize the CDR-R development to begin.

For the first phase's set of features, we employed our traditional waterfall approach: software requirements were developed to meet the system level requirements, and then a design to fulfill the software requirements, then code was developed to implement the design, then testing and integration. This phase completed with a software delivery containing the full scope of planned phase-1 modifications, however the performance of the development effort suffered from cost overruns and internal schedule slippage. Much rework was generated towards the end of the development phase, as we began to test the software and encountered complications when running in the target hardware environment. Several other problems required revisiting the requirements, the design, and underlying code implementation. In my opinion, at the root of these issues were two primary root causes: Unclear/uncertain requirements, and a delayed ability to test the software.

These two issues have a compounding effect on each other: due to the waterfall approach of developing components in isolation of each other, the system functionality that we were trying to achieve only came to being at the tail-end of the development process, when all of the CSCIs (software components) was developed, tested in isolation, then integrated to produce the required functionality. Unfortunately, we typically only reach this point after 3/4ths or more of the schedule, and budgeted effort has been consumed. This may not be problematic if requirements are well-defined, correct, complete, and unambiguous – but here we found this not to be the case. Identifying requirements issues that late in the development process meant several re-water-falling rework iterations of requirements/design/code at the very end of the development cycle when little time was left. Two key project performance measures, Schedule Performance Index (SPI) and Cost Performance Index (CPI), for this phase-1 of development, were 0.82 SPI and 0.76 CPI, meaning that the software was behind schedule by 18% and 24% over cost.

For the second phase, I proposed that we employ an Agile approach to development, based on the Scrum methodology (described later in this research.) Management was receptive to this proposition, and eager to support this effort, especially as the desire to "go agile" was being communicated top-down through the organization, exemplified by a corporate-backed initiative named "SWIFT" (Software Innovation for Tomorrow) that had begun piloting Agile practices on several other large programs in the company. Note that ours was not one of the SWIFT pilot programs, but an organic home-grown desire to employ Agile methods, with prior successes in AIG development and the PrOOD in mind.

A small team of developers was assembled, trained in Scrum methodology, and produced the phase-2 software increment in three sprints of three weeks each. This is relatively fast in an organization where conducting a code inspection alone can eat up a week in development time. Phase-2 thus enjoyed an SPI of 1.07 (7% ahead of schedule), yet the CPI of 0.73 remained less than ideal.

While the Scrum approach helped us beat the schedule, our cost performance did not improve. Several factors could explain this: The team was new to Scrum, required training sessions, and only had the chance to execute three sprints. We did not have a product owner or customer representatives involved, so the requirements were still unclear and conflicting. A new web-based code review tool was deployed during our second sprint, but in retrospect, it was not optimally used and ended up causing wasted effort. We also had to deal with a slew of defects and issues from the phase-1 delivery; in other words, we were building on top of a baseline that still had undiscovered defects. Finally, there was the overhead of trying to fit the agile

Personal Reflections

It is important to note that the activity of "software development" fits within an integrated approach to product development that includes program software development model within an integrated approach to product development team could adopt Scrum. Other parts of the engineering organization, such as System Engineering (SEs, producers of software requirements) and Software Integration and Test (SIs, integrators, and testers of the system) were still operating in a traditional approach, where SEs handoff completed requirements to development, which in turn hand off completed code to SIs.

Since Scrum was adopted just within the confines of software development, and not as a complete IPDP overhaul, this meant that the development team had to maintain the same "interfaces" to the other activities in the program, and had to produce the same work artifacts (e.g., design documentation, review packages), employ the same level of process rigor– all of which was monitored by the Software Quality Assurance (SQA) oversight group. This included holding all of the required inspections and feeding back progress to management, which expected clear Earned Value (EV) based reports of progress.

Yet with all of this, Scrum seemed to energize the development team, produce working code much faster, and speed up the experience gain of new engineers. There was some benefit to Agile. As a result, I decided to pursue this research on Agile development for my graduate thesis in the M.I.T. Systems Design & Management (SDM) program. The research would take a "deep dive" into Agile, and take a close look at agile practices to understand how to integrate them in a CMMI level 5 software engineering environment. During my time at SDM, I also discovered the worlds of Systems Thinking and Systems Dynamics (SD) and found the SD approach to be the best tool for understanding the emergent behavior of a 'complex socio-technical system,' in this case, the software.

AGILE SOFTWARE DEVELOPMENT

In the 1990s, as the large software firms were "maturing" along the CMM dimension, and coinciding with the internet boom and massive growth in the commercial software industry, a parallel movement was taking place: lightweight software development methods, so-called "Agile" methods were evolving, focusing on "soft" factors such as cross-functional teams, customer involvement, and face-to-face communication, collaboration, and creativity. Agile approaches emphasize rapidly building working software, rather than spending much time writing specifications upfront. Agile also is geared towards incremental delivery and frequent iteration, with continuous customer input along the way.

One of the early examples of agile methodologies is eXtreme Programming (XP,) which appeared in the mid-nineties. Extreme Programming emphasizes teamwork. Managers, customers, and developers are all equal partners in a collaborative team. It implements a simple yet effective environment enabling teams to become highly productive. It preaches such practices as pair-programming, automated unit-testing, and incremental development.

In the dot-com era, time-to-market became critical for web-based startups, as the business became an extremely high-velocity environment. The ecosystem of users, needs, and technologies were changing at a break-neck speed. One of the main realizations that came with this was that "change is inevitable, so we might as well embrace it." This goes against the traditional Change-Management approach of locking down requirements and specifications at the outset of a project; however, it was the reality for most software developers in the commercial realm.

In February 2001, a group of experienced software professionals, representing practices ranging from Extreme Programming to SCRUM, and others sympathetic to the need for an alternative to heavyweight software development processes, convened in Utah. They formed the Agile Alliance, and what emerged was the "Agile Manifesto."

HOW TO TURN YOUR ORGANIZATION AGILE AND GET ALL THE BENEFITS OUT OF AGILE SOFTWARE DEVELOPMENT

Over the years, the software development process has seen various enhancements. From the traditional waterfall model to Agile development methodology, companies have upgraded their software development practices to ensure that the final product meets the requirements of the clients and includes the best-in-class features.

Organizations realize many benefits by adopting Agile as the methodology for software development. Different types of Agile methodologies like Scrum, Lean, Kanban, Feature Driven Development, etc., are being favored by companies across the world to deliver better and more efficient services.

Before digging into the benefits, let us briefly understand what exactly Agile is.

Agile is a set of principles that apply iterative techniques in developing software and allow teams to change their mindset towards building a better product. Getting feedback from the customers throughout the cycle helps in fixing defects and avoids the cost of rework.

Benefits of Agile Methodology

Let us deal with the various benefits which Agile has to offer for the organizations:

- **Encourages Adaptability**

Companies get a competitive advantage if their teams are capable of responding to changes quickly and adapt to new processes as required. The Agile methodology encourages flexibility over the plans and processes so that any change does not disturb the project cycle. It helps team members to become creative and learn how to deliver effective solutions in a changing environment.

- **Key to Great Customer Experience**

Agile methodologies like Scrum involve customers throughout the project and address their changing needs by adopting an iterative approach. Gathering feedback constantly from the client helps in aligning the processes with their **business** goals. This is in contrast to the Waterfall method wherein the customer doesn't have any idea about the progress until the final product is developed.

- **Increased Transparency Among Teams**

  Agile methodologies encourage communication between teams so that they have a common goal to achieve. There is increased transparency among product owner, development team, and scrum master as they hold discussions through daily scrum meetings. Regular sprint reviews allow members of the project team to understand how the work progress is at any given time.

- **Early Identification of Problems**

  One of the benefits of Agile methodology is that problems are identified at an early stage. As regular testing is integrated during the cycle, testers can identify bugs, and the developers can address them right away without this affecting the planned work. This way, problems will decrease in subsequent sprints.

- **The Final Product Contains the Most Useful Features**

Better team collaboration, daily testing of the code, discussing possible issues during sprint meetings, having clarity on business goals, and incorporating the changing business needs leads to an efficient final product. The final product evolves after addressing all of the needs and brings in all the useful features that lead to a happy customer.

- **Low Probability of Project Failure**

There are hardly any chances of complete project failure when organizations adopt Agile methodologies for software development. As the project work is reviewed after each sprint, the teams can understand if their approach is bringing the desired results. Regular communication between the development team, scrum master, and the product owner ensures that feedbacks are taken into account to improve the functionality.

- **Final Words**

The benefits discussed above are the primary reasons why organizations have adopted Agile methodologies for their projects. This has led to an increase in demand for professionals who have an in-depth understanding of Agile principles and how can they be applied.

One of the best ways in which individuals validate their knowledge in Agile is by pursuing Agile and Scrum certifications that are industry-wide recognized. Many prestigious institutions offer certifications in Agile like EXIN, Scrum Alliance, Scrum.org, Project Management Institute (PMI), International Consortium for Agile, Scaled Agile Academy, etc., to name a few.

Achieving a Scrum Master Certification London can prove to be highly beneficial as their demand is rising rapidly all over the world. Some of the most sought after Agile certifications are:

- Agile Scrum Master (ASM®)
- Certified ScrumMaster® (CSM)
- PMI-ACP® (Agile Certified Practitioner)
- CSPO Certification

- SAFe® Agilist

Every Agile certification comes with a set of prerequisites that individuals need to fulfill before becoming eligible to achieve them. For some certifications, it is mandatory to attend training and then pass the associated exam apart from having a certain level of experience.

For example, candidates need to attend 16 hours of scrum master training if they wish to pursue a CSM certification. Undergoing Agile training can help professionals gain a thorough knowledge of all the essential concepts and prepare them for achieving such certification. So, begin your Agile journey today and pave the way for a promising career ahead.

PRINCIPLES OF AGILE AND MORE ABOUT AGILE MANIFESTO

The Twelve Agile Principles

The Twelve Principles are the guiding principles for the methodologies that are included under the title "The Agile Movement." They describe a culture in which change is welcome, and the customer is the focus of the work. They also demonstrate the movement's intent, as expressed by Alistair Cockburn, one of the signatories to the Agile Manifesto, which is to align development with business needs.

The twelve principles of agile development include:

- **Customer satisfaction through early and continuous software delivery** – Customers are happier when they receive working software at regular intervals, rather than waiting extended periods between releases.

- **Accommodate changing requirements throughout the development process** – The ability to avoid delays when a requirement or feature request changes.

- **Frequent delivery of working software** – Scrum accommodates this principle since the team operates in software sprints or iterations that ensure regular delivery of working software.

- **Collaboration** between the business stakeholders and developers throughout the project– Better decisions are made when the business and technical team are aligned.

- **Support, trust, and motivate the people involved** – Motivated teams are more likely to deliver their best work than unhappy groups.

- **Enable face-to-face interactions** – Communication is more successful when development teams are co-located.

- **Working software is the primary measure of progress** – Delivering functional software to the customer is the ultimate factor that measures progress.

- **Agile processes to support a consistent development pace** – Teams establish a repeatable and maintainable speed at which they can deliver working software, and they repeat it with each release.

- **Attention to technical detail and design enhances agility** – The right skills and functional design ensures the team can maintain the pace, continually improve the product, and sustain change.

- **Simplicity** – Develop just enough to get the job done for right now.

- **Self-organizing teams encourage great architectures, requirements, and designs** – Skilled and motivated team members who have decision-making power, take ownership, communicate regularly with other team members, and share ideas that deliver quality products.

- **Regular reflections on how to become more productive** – Self-improvement, process improvement, advancing skills, and techniques help team members work more efficiently.

Agile intends to align development with business needs, and the success of Agile is apparent. Agile projects are customer-focused and encourage customer guidance and participation. As a result, Agile has grown to be an overarching view of software development throughout the software industry and an industry all by itself.

AGILE MANIFESTO

The Four Values of the Agile Manifesto:

The Agile Manifesto is comprised of four foundational values and 12 supporting principles that lead the Agile approach to software development. Each Agile methodology applies the four values in different ways, but all of them rely on them to guide the development and delivery of high-quality, working software.

1. Individuals and Interactions over Processes and Tools

The first value in the Agile Manifesto is "Individuals and interactions over processes and tools." Valuing people more highly than processes or tools is easy to understand because it is the people who respond to business needs and drive the development process. If the process or the tools drive development, the team is less responsive to change and less likely to meet customer needs. Communication is an example of the difference between valuing individuals versus process. In the case of individuals, communication is fluid and happens when a need arises. In the case of a process, communication is scheduled and requires specific content.

2. Working Software over Comprehensive Documentation

Historically, enormous amounts of time were spent on documenting the product for development and final delivery. Technical specifications, technical requirements, technical prospectus, interface design documents, test plans, documentation plans, and approvals are required for each. The list was extensive and was a cause for the long delays in development. Agile does not eliminate documentation, but it streamlines it in a form that gives the developer what is needed to do the work without getting bogged down in minutiae. The Agile Manifesto values documentation, but it values working software more.

3. Customer Collaboration over Contract Negotiation

Negotiation is the period when the customer and the product manager work out the details of delivery, with points along the way where the circumstances may be renegotiated. Collaboration is a different creature entirely. With development models such as Waterfall, customers negotiate the requirements for the product, often in great detail, before any work starts. This meant the customer was involved in the process of development before development began and after it was completed, but not during the process. The Agile Manifesto describes a customer who is engaged and collaborates throughout the development process, making. This makes it far easier for developers to meet the needs of the customer. Agile methods may include the customer at intervals for periodic demos, but a project could just as quickly have an end-user as a daily part of the team and attending all meetings, ensuring the product meets the business needs of the customer.

4. Responding to Change Over Following a Plan

Traditional software development regarded change as an expense, so it was to be avoided. The intention was to develop detailed, elaborate plans, with a defined set of features and with everything, generally, having as high a priority as everything else, and with a large number of many dependencies on delivering in a particular order so that the team can work on the next piece of the puzzle.

With Agile, the shortness of an iteration means priorities can be shifted from repetition to iteration, and new features can be added into the next iteration. Agile's view is that changes always improve a project; changes provide additional value.

Perhaps nothing illustrates Agile's positive approach to change better than the concept of Method Tailoring, defined in An Agile Information Systems Development Method in use as: "A process or capability in which human agents determine a system development approach for a specific project situation through responsive changes in, and dynamic interplays between contexts, intentions, and method fragments." Agile methodologies allow the Agile team to modify the process and make it fit the group rather than the other way around.

HOW TO APPLY AGILE PRINCIPLES OF PROJECT MANAGEMENT

Agile principles are explicitly designed to increase the success of your projects. Agility in project management encompasses three key areas:

- Making sure the development team can be productive and can sustainably increase productivity over long periods.

- Ensuring that information about the project's progress is available to stakeholders without interrupting the flow of development activities by asking the development team for updates.

- Handling requests for new features as they occur and integrating them into the product development cycle.

An Agile approach focuses on planning and executing the work to produce the best product that can be released. The approach is supported by communicating openly, avoiding distractions and wasteful activities, and ensuring that the progress of the project is clear to everyone.

All 12 principles support project management, but principles 2, 8, and 10 stands out:

(2) Welcome changing requirements, even late in development. Agile processes harness change for the customer's competitive advantage.

(8) Agile processes promote sustainable development. The sponsors, developers, and users should be able to maintain a constant pace indefinitely.

(10) Simplicity — the art of maximizing the amount of work not done — is essential.

TECHNIQUES YOU CAN UTILIZE IN ORDER TO GET THE MOST OUT OF AGILE SOFTWARE DEVELOPMENT

Here are seven elements of agile you can apply to your projects - along with advice on how to tailor these to suit your specific requirements - to ensure you remain ahead of the curve and extract the maximum value from the methodology.

1. Iterative planning

The key to Agile's increased flexibility is an iterative approach to planning. Essentially, this means that instead of creating a comprehensive blueprint at the outset of a project (when understanding is at its lowest), planning happens continuously, through a process of on-going inspection and adaptation. This enables the direction of the project to change and evolve as understanding grows, and further details of requirements emerge, as well as in response to current market conditions, stakeholder input, and user feedback.

In a marketing context, some initiatives benefit from iterative planning. By incorporating regular reviews into an on-going promotional campaign, for example, you'll be able to quickly drop activities that aren't yielding results and instead re-invest in more productive areas. You could also apply an agile approach to an upcoming product launch, reviewing the priority of associated tasks as new requirements come to light.

For a practical demonstration of iterative planning, check out this version of the popular game of battleships, which shows how the approach works and the benefits it offers.

2. Iterative delivery

As with planning, the Agile approach to delivery is also iterative and focuses on the completion of individual features and tasks so that projects can go live at virtually any point as a lightweight deliverable or Minimum Viable Product (MVP). Different agile frameworks manage iterative delivery in different ways, though, and the one that best suits you will depend on the specific requirements of your organization and industry.

You may, for example, want to adopt a Scrum approach, where work is completed in short and contained stages known as 'sprints.' Typically lasting two weeks, working features are delivered and demonstrated to stakeholders at the end of every sprint, to speed up feedback loops, minimize wasted investment, and provide greater control over budgets.

In the Kanban framework, by contrast, a prioritized list of tasks (or 'backlog') is used to manage activity, with limits placed on work in progress to ensure that the most valuable items are delivered first and those bottlenecks are identified and resolved at an early stage.

Of course, you could also adopt a hybrid model that combines these two approaches - choosing specific aspects from each to create something that's uniquely tailored to your needs.

3. User stories

While not exclusive to the approach, user stories do align closely with Agile's core principles and can help maximize the value being delivered through your projects.

User stories take the form "As [user], I want to [task], so that [motivation]", which ensures that requirements are expressed with direct reference to the user needs that are being fulfilled, and also makes them ideal for communicating these requirements to all relevant project stakeholders in a format that's clear and easy-to-understand.

If this specific format doesn't work for you, though, what matters is that you communicate requirements in a way that maintains the qualities of a good user story. The INVEST mnemonic can prove useful here:

- Independent

- Negotiable

- Valuable

- Estimable

- Small

- Testable

Tasks may, therefore, be "draft a blog post," "identify valuable PPC terms," or "present the business case for a new strategic investment" - but there's no limit to their potential diversity.

4. Estimation and prioritization

Breaking your requirements down into clear, contained user stories (or similar tasks) will make it much easier to assess the effort needed to complete each unit of work, supporting and streamlining any subsequent estimation activities. Additionally, agile promotes a range of techniques to help safeguard the accuracy of estimates, such as planning poker and affinity estimation.

Once estimated, you'll also want to prioritize your stories according to business value, although, of course, exactly how this value is defined will depend on your specific goals and objectives. However, you choose to prioritize, though; it's essential that - in line with Agile's iterative process - you regularly review your prioritized list as your project progresses.

This will deliver you a backlog of tasks that are always up-to-date so that you can be confident the most valuable features are being worked on at all times. It also enables you to amend your backlog in response to any feedback received - which leads me nicely on to.

5. Demonstrations, retrospectives, and stand-ups

Providing team members and the full stakeholder group with the chance to regularly assess project progress, presentations, retrospectives, and stand-ups are all critical features of the Scrum framework. Let's look at each of these in turn:

- These occur at the end of every sprint and involve both the core project team and those stakeholders that may not be directly involved in the day-to-day running of the project. As such, they offer the chance to capture feedback that can then be used to inform subsequent prioritization and delivery activities, as well as acting as a valuable project check-point.

- These also take place following the completion of each sprint, but rather than focusing on the project deliverables instead allow the project team to reflect on their performance - identifying what is working well alongside any areas for improvement.

- **Stand-ups.** Stand-ups occur daily throughout the sprint and allow team members to share what they achieved the previous day, what they're going to work on next, and any blockers they may be facing, to help maintain project momentum and foster high levels of visibility.

6. Communication and collaboration

While the techniques listed so far all undoubtedly offer value to organizations both within and beyond the software development industry, genuinely unlocking the power of agile requires a cultural shift right across your team or teams. Fostering effective collaboration, in particular, is vital, as this will provide you with the insight needed to keep activity aligned with your strategic goals and ensure you're addressing real-world requirements and use contexts.

It's essential, therefore, to look at how well your team communicates and works together currently and put in place any training activities to ensure they have both the understanding and skills needed to manage these activities. Additionally, tools such as instant messaging systems and project management solutions can also support productive communication (although face-to-face will always be one of the most effective channels!), and you may wish to consider introducing testing activities into your processes, to give you end-user feedback at an early stage.

7. Team structures and roles

To ensure projects are delivered as efficiently as possible, many agile frameworks recommend limiting core team size to between three and six, a model that can help numerous industries to maintain focus and velocity. Traditionally, of course, this 'core team' referred to developers producing web and software solutions, but can be applied to anything from salespeople making calls through to content strategists defining and providing the copy.

There are also typically several additional functions surrounding this core team that it may be beneficial to introduce (you can even assign these roles to existing team members, provided they're informed of the scope of and reasons behind their responsibilities):

- **Product Owner.** The Product Owner is responsible for making sure that the work being completed delivers the most significant possible value to the end-users, and maintaining this user focus throughout the project.

- **Scrum Master.** This is a particularly important role for sprint-based approaches, as Scrum Masters help optimize team performance by removing those blockers identified in the daily stand-up, alongside working with other stakeholders to ensure the core team is adequately supported.

The presence of these two roles does not mean, however, that the team should be micro-managed. Indeed, the goal should be to build teams that are empowered to take ownership of tasks and make decisions while maintaining on-going communication and collaboration to keep the project aligned with your strategic goals.

Next steps

Hopefully, I've convinced you to explore further some of the agile techniques introduced in this post. Before you begin your agile transformation journey, however, it's vital that you underpin it with a clearly-defined strategy, and the following tasks can help you to achieve this:

- Conduct an 'as-is' audit

- Identify the most appropriate approach for you

- Create a training plan

- Implement a trial project/period

- Roll out across your organization

COMMON CHALLENGES OF IMPLEMENTING AGILE METHOD

Challenges of Agile Development

Although there are many benefits of Agile software development, there are also several common challenges that prevent many teams from successfully scaling Agile processes out to the enterprise level. In Forrester's State of Agile 2017: Agile at Scale development study, both large and small firms cited the following as the top 3 barriers to Agile adoption:

1. People's behavioral change:

Changing the way people work is difficult — the habits and culture of a large development organization are typically profoundly ingrained. People naturally resist change, and when confronted with an Agile transformation, you may often hear people say things like, "that's the way we've always done it around here," or "that won't work here." Accepting change means accepting the possibility that you might not currently be doing things the best way, or even worse, it may challenge a person's long-held values. It's easy for people to keep their old behaviors and processes—unless there is an excellent reason to make a change.

2. Lack of skilled product owners from the business side:

The Business Requirements Document (BRD) has been used for decades. Yes, it has its shortcomings, but it's familiar. Most of the people involved in requirements – primarily business stakeholders and Business Analysts (BAs) – are new to Agile. They don't understand user stories and hesitate to give up the BRD for something different because they view it as a contract between them and IT. How will they be able to control the direction of development without that contract?

Additionally, most Agile software development teams use an ALM tool, which is where user stories need to end up for decomposition into development tasks. Most business stakeholders and BAs, on the other hand, still use Microsoft Word and Excel to author requirements. This tool mismatch stifles the cross-departmental collaboration teams need to realize the full benefits of Agile.

3. Lack of dedicated cross-functional teams:

The language used in the principles behind the Agile Manifesto—which refer to the technical members of the Agile team as "developers"—has led many to think that only developers, or what many people think of as 'coders,' are needed within an Agile team. However, the Manifesto's guidelines use the word developer to mean "product developer"—any cross-functional role that helps the team deliver the product.

According to the Scrum Guide, a cross-functional team is a team that is organized around customer value stream mapping and must include all competencies needed to accomplish their work without depending on others that are not part of the team. These teams deliver products iteratively and incrementally, maximizing opportunities for feedback, and ensuring a potentially useful version of working product is always available.

Looking for a Tool to Support your Agile Software Development Efforts?

Storyteller helps you easily plan and track your Agile software projects, releases, and iterations with drag-and-drop simplicity using an intuitive user interface. Storyteller synchronizes with downstream ALM and test management tools to enable enterprise-scale Agile by automating and orchestrating business-driven goals and measures into the software development lifecycle.

Backlog items can be planned for the next iteration, providing the opportunity to introduce changes within a few weeks.

UNDERSTANDING THE AGILE METHODOLOGY AND HOW TO USE IT

Agile Methodology is a people-focused, results-focused approach to software development that respects our rapidly changing world. It's centered around adaptive planning, self-organization, and short delivery times. It's flexible, fast, and aims for continuous improvements in quality, using tools like *Scrum* and *eXtreme Programming.*

How It Works

It works by first admitting that the old "waterfall" method of software development leaves a lot to be desired. The process of "plan, design, build, test, deliver," works okay for making cars or buildings but not as well for creating software systems. In a business environment where hardware, demand, and competition are all swiftly-changing variables, agile works by walking the fine line between too much process and not enough.

Agile Methodology Overview

It abandons the risk of spending months or years on a process that ultimately fails because of some small mistake in an early phase. It relies instead on trusting employees and teams to work directly with customers to understand the goals and provide solutions in a fast and incremental way.

- **Faster, smaller.** Traditional software development relied on phases like outlining the requirements, planning, design, building, testing, and delivery. Agile methodology, by contrast, looks to deploy the first increment in a couple of weeks and the entire piece of software in a couple of months.
- **Communication**. Agile teams within the business work together daily at every stage of the project through face-to-face meetings. This collaboration and communication ensure the process stays on track even as conditions change.
- **Feedback**. Rather than waiting until the delivery phase to gauge success, teams leveraging Agile methodology track the progress and speed of the development process regularly. Velocity is measured after the delivery of each increment.
- **Trust**. Agile teams and employees are self-organizing. Rather than following a manifesto of rules from management *intended* to produce the desired

result, they understand the goals and create their path to reach them.

- **Adjust**. Participants tune and adjust the process continually, following the KIS or **Keep It Simple** principle.

For training purposes, there's a comprehensive, downloadable overview here.

Examples of Agile Methodology

The most popular and typical examples are Scrum, eXtreme Programming (XP), Feature Driven Development (FDD), Dynamic Systems Development Method (DSDM), Adaptive Software Development (ASD), Crystal, and Lean Software Development (LSD). Teams generally pick one or two methods. The most widely used methodologies are Scrum and XP, which dovetail nicely.

Scrum is a hands-on system consisting of simple interlocking steps and components:

- A product owner makes a prioritized wish list known as a product backlog.

- The *scrum team* takes one small piece of the top of the wish list called a *sprint backlog* and plans to implement it.
- The team completes their sprint backlog task in a *sprint* (2 weeks). They assess progress in a meeting called a *daily scrum.*
- The *ScrumMaster* keeps the team focused on the goal.
- At the sprint's end, the work is ready to ship or show. The team closes the sprint with a review, then starts newsprint.

Here's an example of how Scrum works: Bill meets with a customer to discuss her company's needs. Those needs are the product backlog. Bill chooses the most important tasks to work on in the next two weeks. His team meets in a daily scrum to target work for the day ahead and address roadblocks. At the end of the sprint, Bill delivers the work, reviews the backlog, and sets the goal for the next sprint. The cycle repeats until the software is complete.

SCRUM PROCESS

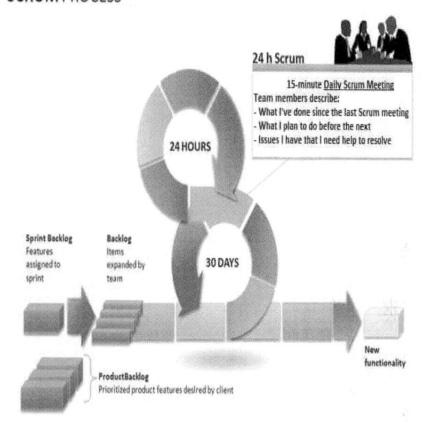

Extreme Programming

Extreme Programming, also referred to as XP, is a lightweight methodology for small-to-medium-sized teams developing software in the face of vague or rapidly changing requirements (Beck 1999). Like Scrum, it emphasizes iterative and incremental delivery of small releases, as depicted in the XP project flowchart

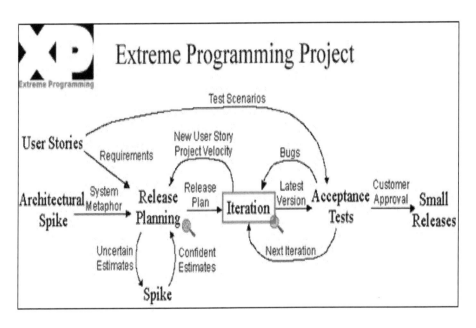

The XP Development Flowchart

eXtreme Programming. Often used with scrum, XP is an example of how Agile can heighten customer satisfaction. Rather than deliver everything the customer could ever want far in the future, it gives them what they need now, fast. XP is centered on frequent releases and short development cycles. It uses a code review, pair programming, unit testing, and regular communication with the customer.

Here's an example of how XP works: Bill builds a list of customer requirements by having the customer tell "user stories" that outline the features. From there, he creates a software release plan. The software will be delivered in iterations, with one delivered every couple of weeks. The team works in programmer pairs, using daily meetings to smooth roadblocks. The customer provides feedback in the form of more user stories. The cycle repeats until the software is delivered.

The following rules govern the development practices of XP teams:

☐ **The Planning Game:** Quickly determine the scope of the next release by combining business priorities and technical estimates. As reality overtakes the plan, update the plan.

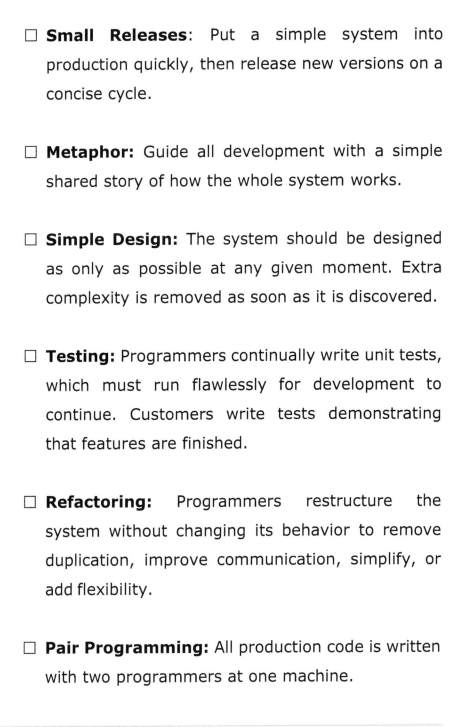

☐ **Small Releases**: Put a simple system into production quickly, then release new versions on a concise cycle.

☐ **Metaphor:** Guide all development with a simple shared story of how the whole system works.

☐ **Simple Design:** The system should be designed as only as possible at any given moment. Extra complexity is removed as soon as it is discovered.

☐ **Testing:** Programmers continually write unit tests, which must run flawlessly for development to continue. Customers write tests demonstrating that features are finished.

☐ **Refactoring:** Programmers restructure the system without changing its behavior to remove duplication, improve communication, simplify, or add flexibility.

☐ **Pair Programming:** All production code is written with two programmers at one machine.

- [ ] **Continuous Integration:** Integrate and build the system many times a day, every time a task is completed.

- [ ] **Collective Ownership:** Anyone can change any code anywhere in the system at any time.

- [ ] **On-site Customer:** Include a real, live client on the team, available full-time to answer questions.

- [ ] ***40 Hour Week***: Never work any more than forty hours a week like a rule. Never work overtime a second week in a row.

- [ ] **Coding Standards:** Programmers write all code by rules emphasizing communication through the code.

Test-Driven Development

Inspired by the "test-first" philosophy from XP, Test Driven Development

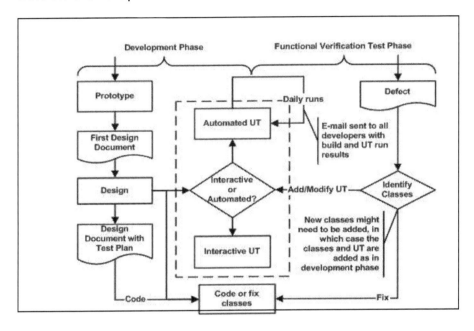

(TDD) starts the development process by coding automated test cases for the software features that are to be produced. Then, the production code is developed iteratively until all the tests are passed. After each cycle (iteration), all of the tests are re-run to ensure that new functionality is well integrated. Refactoring is performed to maintain quality and remove duplication in both production and test code. The Figure above illustrates this process as practiced by a software development group at IBM (Maximilien & Williams 2003).

TDD's test-first approach is reported to have a significant impact on defect prevention, but more importantly, it influences the design of the software. Since developers must focus on the interfaces of their modules (this helps in developing modules to pass the unit tests), it means that they must employ a type of "Design by Contract" (often referred to as the "DbC") approach to software development. Test-first code tends to be more cohesive and less coupled than code in which testing isn't part of the intimate coding cycle (Beck 2001). In a nutshell, Kent Beck, the creator of XP and TDD, lists the benefits of a test-first approach as follows:

- Encourages you to be explicit about the scope of the implementation.

- It helps separate logical design from physical design from implementation.

- Help grow your confidence in the correct functioning of the system as the system grows.

- Help simplify your designs.

Feature Driven Development

Feature Driven Development (FDD) is described as having "just enough process to ensure scalability and repeatability and encourage creativity and innovation all along the way" (Highsmith 2002a). FDD breaks the system into feature sets, and iterates to produce incremental client-valued pieces of functionality. Its eight "best practices can summarize FDD":

- **Domain object modeling:** Since FDD was developed initially in 1997 for a Java language-based project, it is tailored to an Object-Oriented (OO) approach. FDD calls for building class diagrams to capture the attributes and relationships between the significant objects in the problem space.
- **Developing By Feature:** The system is broken up in a set of features that can be developed incrementally. In FDD, an element is a small, client valued function that can be implemented in two weeks (Goyal 2007).
- **Individual class ownership:** Unlike XP, which calls for "collective code ownership," FDD asks that each class (a unit of code in OO programming) is

assigned to an individual who is ultimately responsible for it.

- **Feature teams:** Features are developed by teams comprised of feature owners and a combination of the class owners needed to implement the given feature.
- **Inspections:** formal code reviews are held to prevent defects and ensure quality.
- **Regular builds:** Allows early detection of integration problems and makes sure there is always a current build available to demo to the customer.
- **Reporting and visibility of results:** Progress for each feature is based on the completion of development milestones (e.g., Design completion, Design Inspection Completion, etc.) The progress of the feature sets is regularly reported.

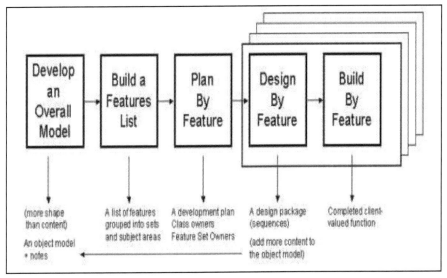

Stages of Feature Driven Development

FDD is similar to the "agile modeling" methodology since it relies on a UML (Unified Modeling Language) model of the system.

Crystal Methods

On a quest to develop an effective software methodology, Alistair Cockburn interviewed and studied project teams for ten years. He found that "people-centric methodologies" do better than "process-centric" methodologies, and that one must choose and tailor the methodology to the team and the assignment - no methodology fits all projects. (Cockburn 2004)

The result is Crystal, which is a family of methods, rather than a single methodology, developed to address the variability between projects. Projects are sized along two dimensions: team size, and program criticality. A version of Crystal is subsequently chosen and adapted to the specifics of the project.

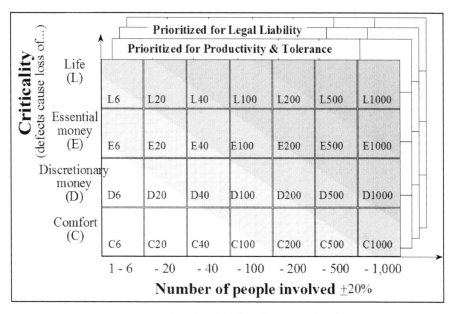

The Crystal family of methods

Team Size accounts for the fact that as a team gets more enormous communication costs to rise and face to face communication becomes less effective. More management and coordination become required. Criticality, on the other hand, measures the system's "potential for causing damage," ranging from "loss of life" to "loss of comfort." The combination of team size and the criticality directs a given development effort towards a corresponding Crystal methodology. Two rules govern the practice of the Crystal family of methods.

- Incremental cycles cannot exceed four months.
- Reflection workshops must be held after every delivery so that the methodology is self- adapting.

Crystal "focuses on people, interaction, community, skills, talents, and communication as first-order effects on performance. The process remains important but secondary" (Highsmith 2002a).

The Agile Genome

After review and analysis of many Agile methodologies, some of which were described earlier, we come to find that they all share common characteristics. The project teams that employ these methodologies, in effect, practice a variety of remarkably similar "Agile techniques."

When seeking to identify the basic set of shared attributes that these Agile methodologies share, we can start to develop a set of characteristics that we can call "the Genome of Agile" – We have distilled these into the following seven genes.

Story/Feature Driven

A principle of the Agile Alliance is "Working software is the primary measure of progress." Most Agile teams break up their projects into manageable sets of "features," "stories," "use cases," or "capabilities," rather than architecting the complete system upfront as is done in classic Big Design Up Front (BDUF) approaches. The terminology differs across the various methodologies, but the concept is the same. Feature Driven Development is perhaps the most obvious example of such a methodology, as it involves building a feature list, then planning, designing, and implementing the software feature by feature. Note that not all features are equal in size, complexity, or priority. In most agile methodologies, features are sized or weighted depending on an estimate of the amount of effort required to implement the feature. Feature planning activities must also take into account feature inter-dependencies and plan accordingly.

From a management perspective, the implication of using this approach is that management can have a concrete measure of progress by-feature (i.e., 9 out of 10 features implemented means 90% complete, assuming all features weighted equally.) This differs from traditional EVM-like measures of progress, based on arguably arbitrary milestones, where, for example, the completion of the design phase translates to claiming forty percent of the project complete. One of the problems with using a waterfall method paired with EVM management methodology is that a project can report being at 90% completion yet still have no functioning software.

Another advantage of the feature-driven approach is that, as features are developed and integrated into the software, they become available for early customer demonstrations as well as early integration and test activities – all of which help reduce uncertainty and detect defects early in the development cycle, as opposed to waiting for a complete integrated build.

The downside of a featured approach is that over time, the software's architecture and code start to exhibit signs of having "high coupling" and "low cohesion," making it harder (and more costly) to maintain and evolve. Coupling refers to the degree to which software modules, components, etc., depend on each other – in a system with high coupling, there is a high degree of dependency, meaning that changes to one software element are likely to have ripple effects and impact on the behavior of other elements. Cohesion is a determinant of how strongly related the responsibilities of a single software module or component are – low coherence is an indicator of lack of structure in the system. (For example, a software library or component that provides a broad set of entirely unrelated functions or services is said to exhibit low cohesion, whereas one that only provides explicitly string manipulation functions is said to be highly cohesive.) The segmentation of a system by feature can lead to "high coupling" and "low cohesion." Higher coupling and lower cohesions mean that there are many software interdependencies; changes to one area of the software will have more impact on other parts of the system and thus makes future changes more costly and challenging to make. This is why Refactoring is called for by most feature-driven methods.

Iterative-Incremental

Another principle of the Agile Alliance is to "deliver working software frequently, from a couple of weeks to a couple of months." Development is performed in repeated cycles (iterative) and portions at a time (incremental.) This allows developers to:

- Take advantage of what was learned during earlier development in later iterations.
- Focus on short term objectives.

In this approach, the development will start with a simple implementation of a subset of the software requirements and iteratively enhance the evolving versions until the full system is implemented. With each iteration, design modifications are made, and new functional capabilities are added. Most value is derived when iterations are designed such that early tasks help resolve uncertainty later in the project. Rather than one big design phase, one big code phase, then one big test phase, here many iterations are performed, with each iteration consisting of a short design-code-test cycle.

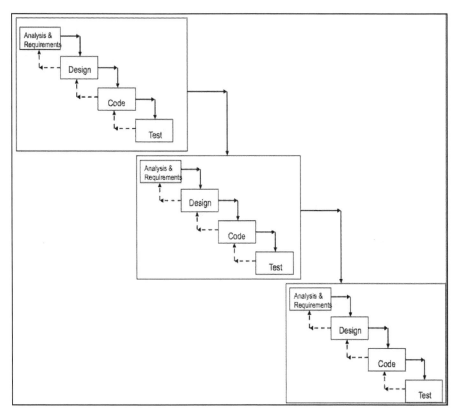

Design-Code-Test iterations (de Weck, & Lyneis 2011)

This "Iterative-Incremental" characteristic combines with the afore-mentioned "feature-driven" gene, to allow the software product to continually evolve as a series of product increments, each one adding more features to the existing software product.

The Iterative-Incremental concept is not novel nor unique to Agile methodologies. There is well-documented evidence of extensive Incremental Iterative Development (IID) for major software development efforts dating back to the sixties (Larman & Basili 2003). Software historians seem to agree that Royce's original work on the Waterfall has been misrepresented as calling for a single iteration of the Waterfall and that he proposed several iterations of the process.

In 1994 the DoD's Defense Science Board Task Force on Acquiring Defense Software Commercially issued a report that stated, "DoD must manage programs using iterative development. Apply evolutionary development with the rapid deployment of initial functional capability." (Larman & Basili 2003).

The result was a new standard for software acquisition introduced that same year, Mil-Std-498, which stated:

"If a system is developed in multiple builds, its requirements may not be adequately defined until the final build [...] If a system is designed in multiple builds, its design may not be fully defined until the final build".

This allowed projects to start while only needing fully-defined requirements for one build at a time, rather than a full requirements specification for the entire project, allowing later requirements analysis efforts to be informed by work and experience from earlier build – a step in the agile direction. This standard, although later replaced by others, was a first attempt to introduce the concept of the lifecycle and incremental delivery to government software projects. It is also an acknowledgment of the fact that Waterfall development and acquisition was problematic, and that the previous DoD standards had a "Waterfall bias" (perceived preference towards a single-pass Waterfall model of development.)

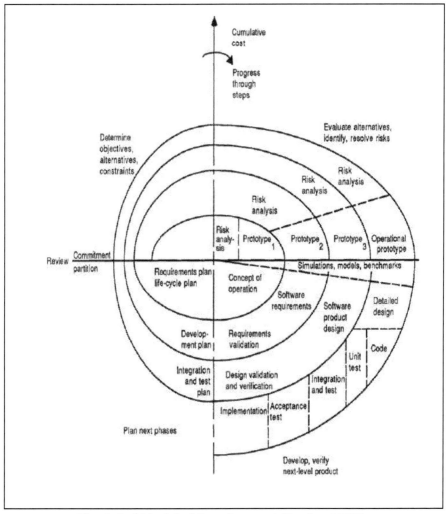

The Spiral Model of Development (Boehm 1987)

Explicit iteration and incremental development are neither new nor unique to Agile. It first came to the forefront of the software engineering community's conscience in 1986 with Barry Boehm's "*A Spiral Model of Software Development and Enhancement.*" The Spiral model, shown above, very simply put, calls for repeated waterfall iterations to build and refine a software product. Early spirals can achieve goals of producing quick-to-market prototypes that can be tested or presented to customers for early feedback, which provides valuable information for later spirals. This approach mitigates project risk and allows requirements to be evolved and refined incrementally, keeping the project agile in that software is built progressively and that the approach caters to the reality of changing requirements.

In 2002, the DoD declared "Evolutionary acquisition strategies shall be preferred approach to satisfying operational needs" and "Spiral development shall be the preferred process" The following two acquisition models became the official standards:

- Incremental Development: The end-state requirement is known, and the requirement will be met over time in several increments.

- Spiral Development: End-state requirements are not known at Program Initiation. Requirements for future increments dependent upon technology maturation and user feedback from initial increments.

Illustrative Example

To illustrate the difference between Iterative Incremental Story Feature-driven approaches vs. a Waterfall/BDUF approach, let us consider the following fictional example: Suppose that we are to develop software for an Automated Teller Machine (ATM). The software is required to allow users to check balances, withdraw/deposit money, and transfer funds between accounts. How would the two approaches differ? Albeit contrived and simplified, this example helps clarify the difference.

Waterfall/BDUF

In the Analysis phase, the requirements for the ATM, the system may be documented in a "System Requirements" document as the result of discussions, negotiations, analysis, and compromise between the customer agent and the contractor's system engineer or business analyst. This document is usually named something akin to "System/Subsystem Specifications" (SSS). Once the SSS requirements for the system are "locked-in," the next phase, "Requirements Specification," can begin.

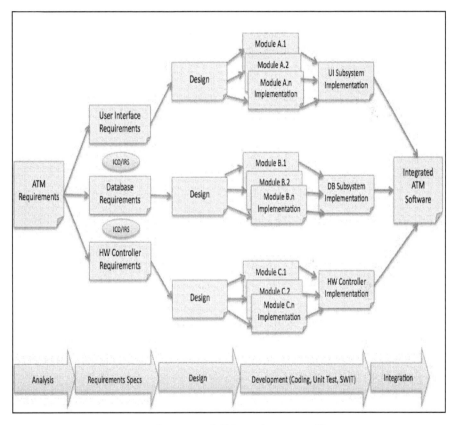

Example Waterfall Development Flow

Using a functional decomposition approach, the next levels of requirements are developed: the architecture is produced, which defines three main subsystems, in this ATM example:

- A User Interface subsystem or component encapsulating the software for interacting with the ATM user.
- A Database component which is responsible for communicating with the bank's central database and accessing account information.
- A Hardware Controller subsystem for interfacing with the actual ATM hardware.

For each subsystem, a "Software Requirements Specification" (SRS) document is produced. Also, interfaces between the subsystems/components are specified in some document, named something like "Interface Requirements Document" (IRS) or "Interface Control Document" (ICD). In theory, if each component meets its SRS requirements and adheres to applicable ICDs, then the system will function as specified in the original SSS.

Next, an individual or team is assigned to the design and development of each subsystem, based on its SRS. A model is produced for each subsystem, followed by the coding of each software module to implement the design. Then, each module is individually tested (Unit Testing.) Once unit testing is completed, the subsystem is tested as a whole, bringing together the individual modules in a "Software Integration and Test" (SWIT) activity. Finally, the component is integrated, and the ATM software system is tested as a whole and validated against the original SSS.

Story/Feature Drive

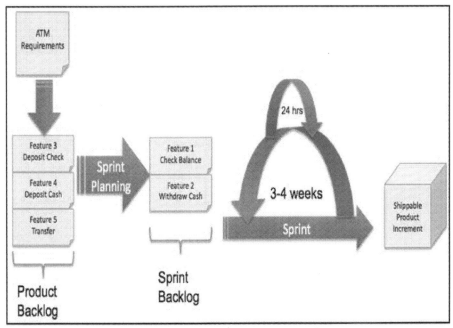

Feature-Driven Scrum Approach

Using a Story/Feature-driven approach, the ATM system is segmented not into functional components, but rather into a set features corresponding to the system's use cases: In this example, the ATM software's list of features may be: Check Balance, Withdraw Cash, Deposit Check, Deposit Cash, and Transfer Balances. Note that in feature-driven approaches, not all features are equal in size or effort. In Scrum, each feature is sized by "story points," a relative measure of the amount of effort estimated to be needed to implement that feature. For this example, let us consider these features equal.

The development team follows by then prioritizing the set of features and starts to develop the software feature-by-feature or a subset of features at a time in short "Sprints." As each sprint is completed, the set of features designed is added as an increment to the software product's baseline producing a "potentially shippable product increment.

Refactoring

An incremental and feature-driven approach to the development of software systems can produce sub-optimal architectures compared to a waterfall model, as discussed previously. One of the advantages of BDUF is that the complete up-front design is optimized for a full-featured release. Components are well-integrated, and duplication is minimized.

On the other hand, refactoring is needed to pay off the "technical/design debt," which accrues over time, especially when incremental and revolutionary design results in a bloated codebase, inflexible architecture, duplication, and other undesirable side effects.

The metaphor of technical debt was used by Ward Cunningham (creator of the Wiki) to describe what happens as the complexity and architecture of a software project grow, and it becomes more and more difficult to make enhancements. The figure below illustrates this concept: as the software product degrades over time, the cost of change increases to the detriment of the customer responsiveness.

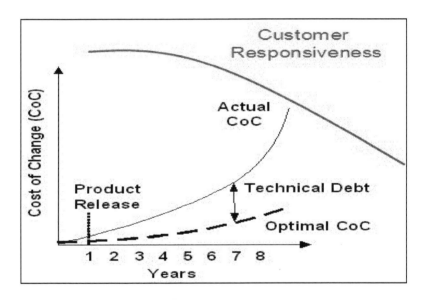

Technical Debt Curve

This concept of technical debt has become popular as both technically minded and business-minded people can understand it. Just like credit debt, technical debt accrues interest payments in the form of extra effort that must be made in subsequent development cycles. Management can choose to pay down the principal on this debt by refactoring, and keep the future cost of change as low as possible.

Controlling the cost of change is very important for an Agile project since the philosophy is to embrace change. Indeed one of the twelve principles of the Agile Manifesto is to welcome changing requirements, even late in development. Agile processes harness change for the customer's competitive advantage. Therefore refactoring is critical to keeping the agile process sustainable through the pay-down of technical debt.

Holistically speaking, one could argue that true Agile is not only about the agility of the development process, or the team, but also about the software product itself. In other words, a "Systems Thinking" perspective would suggest that the software product itself is part of the system under study here, *in addition to* the people, processes, and tools. If the software is continuously refactored to keep it comfortable to adapt and evolve along with the requirements, needs, or market environment, then the project can indeed be agile.

Perhaps one of the problems with Agile adoption in large-scale government programs is with attempting to employ it on long-running legacy programs that are already deep in technical debt.

Many agile methodologies (in particular XP) consider refactoring to be a primary development practice. Refactoring has the disadvantage that it takes extra effort and requires changing baseline software without any direct or apparent ROI. A project manager may ask, "why are we spending effort re-designing portions of the system unrelated to the next planned set of features?" This is when the technical debt metaphor comes in handy as a tool for communicating the business impact of design and architectural decisions.

The project management may still resist refactoring with: "If we do refactoring, we will have to re-test and re-certify existing baseline functionality, at added effort and cost to the project!" Any change has the potential to reduce the maturity and the stability of the software, requiring regression testing and revalidation of the baseline feature set. This is why it is advantageous to practice refactoring in conjunction with text-heavy practices (e.g., TDD) and Continuous Integration techniques.

An example of a software organization that embraces refactoring as part of its software engineering culture is Google. The following points, taken from Google's Agile Training (Mcfarland 2006), summarize some of the reasons behind their embrace of Refactoring:

- As code ages, the cost of change goes up
- As Google grows, the percentage of code in maintenance mode grows with it
- We need to keep code flexible, so we can change it to suit new market conditions quickly
- It's not essential if all you're trying to do is get new products out. (Smart programmers can develop outstanding applications without tests, but those applications will be much harder to maintain.)

A final note on refactoring and technical/design debt is that this phenomenon can be observed at the enterprise level. We find that much of the work in net-centric architecture, which involves evolving an ecosystem of siloed systems towards a system-of-systems architecture using technical approaches such as SOA (Service-Oriented Architecture), can be understood through the lens of technical debt as grand-scale exercises in refactoring.

Micro – Optimizing

This gene represents the adaptive nature of agile processes. We employ the term "Optimizing" because, in most agile methodologies, teams are empowered if not encouraged to modify aspects of the development process or dynamically adapt to changing circumstances. "Micro" is used to indicate that small process adjustments and improvements are made frequently and as needed. For example, the Scrum process requires a "Sprint Retrospective" in between iterations. Likewise, Alistair Cockburn – author of the Crystal methods -- believes that as the project and the people evolve, the methodology so too must be tuned and evolved. Crystal, therefore, calls for reflection workshops to be held after every delivery so that the methodology is self- adapting.

This relates to the concept of Double Loop Learning, as applied to software development: Single Loop learning describes the plan-do-check-adjust cycle where we learn and increase the efficiency of what we are doing. Double Loop learning is when we step back and question our assumptions and goals and revise them.

As an example of this, consider code reviews in a software development organization that has a process in place that calls for software inspections. This process may include an onerous series of tasks such as the manual preparation of code review packages. There are so many components, checklists, and forms required to be part of the package that it may take a developer a whole day (or from a project management perspective, a

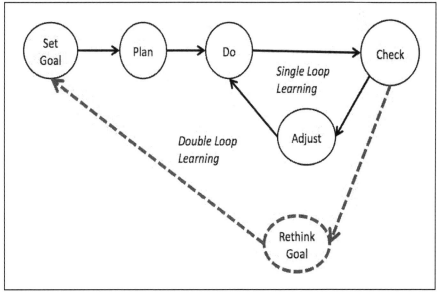

person-day worth of effort) to produce this package. Then perhaps several days elapse before a meeting can be scheduled for all of the necessary players to convene and perform the code review. Finally, action items must be documented, implemented, and verified.

Traditional improvement efforts will focus on automating this process and making it more efficient. The result of single-loop learning may be process enhancements and automation to speed up the code review process for example, by automating the review package generation task.

On the other hand, a team that exhibits characteristics of double-loop learning will question the goal of the inspection process itself. What is the return on investment (ROI), or value-add, that this inspection process brings to the development effort? It may find that the intent is to detect and correct coding defects only. The team may react by eliminating this process altogether and adopting the use of pair programming (as a flavor of real-time code inspection) in conjunction with static analysis tools, and even arrange for customer demonstrations and user involvement events, in a push to even further attain the goal of detecting software defects at the implementation level as well as at the level of system users' needs.

Traditional development approaches, even ones that employ a single-pass waterfall, can exhibit a "light" flavor of this gene: heavyweight processes often call for

Lessons Learned activities after a software project. The problem is that this usually produces a Lessons Learned document that rarely feeds into the next development cycle and has little improvement effect on subsequent development projects. In the context of Agile, however, the sprints are short enough, and retrospectives frequent enough so that process adjustment is near-continuous throughout the life of a project.

Another aspect of many agile methodologies is that teams are often empowered to self-regulate workload. Teams are trusted to self-adjust and gradually learn about how much work they can handle in a given period (e.g., sprint). In Scrum, the measure of "Velocity" or "Sprint Velocity" represents how much product backlog effort can handle in one sprint. It is established on a sprint-by-sprint basis as the team learns about the project and about working with each other. Typically, team velocity improves as sprint cycles are completed and experience gained.

Benefits of Agile Methodology

The benefits of Agile are tied directly to its faster, lighter, more engaged mindset. The process, in a nutshell, delivers what the customer wants when the customer wants it. There's much less wasted time spent developing in the wrong direction, and the entire system is quicker to respond to changes. For a more comprehensive list of benefits,

- **Faster**. Speed is one of the most significant benefits of Agile Methodology. A faster software development life cycle means less time between paying and getting paid. That, in turn, means a more profitable business.

- **It increases customer satisfaction**. With Agile, customers don't wait for months or years, only to get what they didn't want. Instead, they get iterations of something very close to what they want, very fast. The system adjusts quickly to refine the successful customer solution, adapting as it goes to changes in the overall environment.

- **Values employees**. Employees whose ideas are valued are vastly more productive than those who are ordered to follow a set of rules. The Agile Methodology respects employees by giving them the goal, then trusting them to reach it. Since they're the ones with their hands on the controls and the ones who see the obstacles that crop up every day, employees are in the best position to respond to challenges and meet the goals at hand.

- **System eliminates work.** By involving the customer at more than just the phases of requirements and delivery, the project remains on-task and in-tune with customer needs at every step. This means less backtracking and less "out on a limb" time between the time we do the work and the time the customer suggests revisions.

Best Practices

The list of best practices is long and involved, with dozens of tools to pick and choose.

- **Set priorities**. A *product backlog* is a list of prioritized tasks maintained by a *product owner.*
- **Maintain small release cycles.** The product should be released in increments every 2-4 weeks, with stakeholders giving feedback before proceeding.
- **Use pair programming.** Two programmers work side-by-side at a single computer. This technique results in an identical degree of productivity to separate programming but delivers higher quality.

- **Refractor.** Rework code regularly to achieve the same result with greater efficiency and clarity.
- **Use test-driven development.** Code the unit test first to keep the project on task throughout. Test-driven development as an Agile best practice also produces greater employee engagement, since it transforms testing from a tedious grind to a coding challenge.

Agile Methodology Tools

The list below shows some of the best tools on offer.

- **ActiveCollab.** An affordable tool for small businesses, ActiveCollab is easy to use. This software development aid requires little training and provides excellent support.
- **Agilo for Scrum.** Stakeholders get updated automatically on the project's progress with Agilo for Scrum. Features sprint reports and burn down charts for better data mining.
- **Atlassian Jira + Agile.** This powerful project management tool facilitates development by incorporating Scrum, Kanban, and customizable workflows.

- **Pivotal Tracker.** This methodology tool is geared specifically for mobile projects. It's user-friendly after a brief orientation period.
- **Prefix.** This free tool from Stackify provides an instant feedback loop to catch and fix bugs before they can deploy.
- **Retrace**. For a more robust solution complete with monitoring, errors, logs, and more, Stackify's Retrace provides app performance insights from integration to QA to production, at the code level.

Benefits of Agile Development

Agile is a powerful tool for software development. It provides process and efficiency benefits to not only the development team but also many significant business benefits to the organization as a whole. Agile helps product teams deal with many of the most common project pitfalls (such as cost, schedule predictability, and scope creep) in a more controlled manner. By reorganizing and re-envisioning the activities involved in custom software development, Agile achieves those same objectives in a leaner and more business-focused way.

Here are the eight primary benefits of an Agile methodology:

1. Improved Quality

One of the most significant benefits of an Agile framework is improved product quality. By breaking down the project into manageable units, the project team can focus on high-quality development, testing, and collaboration. Also, by producing frequent builds and conducting testing and reviews during each iteration, quality is improved by finding and fixing defects quickly and identifying expectation mismatches early.

By adopting Agile software development practices, organizations can deliver solutions on time and with a higher degree of client and customer satisfaction. By incorporating the ability to change, they are better able to integrate feedback from demos, usability testing, and customers into the product.

2. Focus on Business Value

Another one of the primary benefits of Agile is an increased focus on delivering strategic business value by involving business stakeholders in the development process. By doing so, the team understands what's most famous and can provide the features that give the most business value to their organization.

3. Focus on Users

Agile development uses user stories with business-focused acceptance criteria to define product features. By focusing features on the needs of real users, each element incrementally delivers value, not just an IT component. This also provides the opportunity to beta test software after each Sprint, gaining valuable feedback early in the project and providing the ability to make changes as needed.

4. Stakeholder Engagement

An Agile process offers multiple opportunities for stakeholder and team engagement – before, during, and after each Sprint. By involving the different types of stakeholders in every step of the project, there is a high degree of collaboration between teams. This provides more opportunities for the team to truly understand the business' vision, deliver working software early, and frequently increases stakeholders' trust. Stakeholders are encouraged to be more deeply engaged in a project since trust has been established in the team's ability to deliver high-quality working software.

5. Transparency

Another benefit of Agile software development is that it provides a unique opportunity for clients or customers to be involved throughout the project. This can include prioritizing features, iteration planning, and review sessions, or frequent software builds containing new features. However, this also requires customers to understand that they see a work in progress in exchange for this added benefit of transparency.

6. Early and Predictable Delivery

By using time-boxed, fixed schedule Sprints of 1-4 weeks, new features are delivered quickly and frequently, with a high level of predictability. This also provides the opportunity to release or beta test the software earlier than planned if there is sufficient business value.

7. Predictable Costs and Schedule

Because each Sprint is a fixed duration, the cost is predictable and limited to the amount of work that can be performed by the team in the fixed-schedule time box. Combined with the estimates provided before each Sprint, the company can more readily understand the approximate cost of each feature, which improves decision making about the priority of features and the need for additional iterations.

8. Allows for Change

Lastly, a vital benefit of an Agile methodology is that, unlike a Waterfall model, it allows for change. While the team needs to stay focused on delivering an agreed-to subset of the product's features during each iteration, there is an opportunity to refine and reprioritize the overall product backlog constantly.

THE KEYS YOU NEED TO SUCCESSFULLY IMPLEMENT AGILE IN YOUR BUSINESS

Implementing agile methodologies (Scrum, Kanban, or any of their variations) is a challenge faced by all kinds of organizations, project offices, and managers. The advantages of being gained from this type of method for a significant number of projects are clear, but implementing them is no simple task. At many organizations, their implementation is often met with fear, rejection, and obstacles. Here are a few keys to successfully implementing an agile methodology.

1. Start with the Right Project

It is possible to apply the agile methodologies to almost any type of project, but the successful implementation of these methods does indeed require selecting the right projects, to begin with, to achieve the maximum benefit in the shortest time.

Trying to apply agile methodologies to predictive or

classic projects does not usually lead to good results, as there is a considerable sense of losing control, with teams (and management) tending to revert to methods they already know. In contrast, experimental projects: presenting a lesser defined or highly changeable scope with multidisciplinary teams and needing fast results: provide an excellent opportunity for applying agile methodologies.

2. Clearly define the Team's Role

The role played by a team in classic or predictive projects is significantly different from their role in agile projects. The Project Manager plays a leading role in the former, with control over all aspects of the project, whereas the team has a much more critical role in the latter, and the Project Manager becomes a facilitator of the methodology. It is essential to clearly define the team's part to implement the method correctly.

An agile project requires a multidisciplinary, self-organized, and self-managed team, which is a confidence challenge for many organizations that tend to apply managed and controlled methods. Understanding and building this type of unit is fundamental. If you can build a team that consists of relationships between equals and a shared goal, a large portion of your future success will be guaranteed.

3. Estimation of Effort is still Key

One of the most common problems when implementing agile methodologies believes that estimates no longer need to be made. Even though it is no longer necessary to make an estimate of the whole project, and we can focus on the tasks for the next sprint or those with a higher priority in the product backlog, it is essential to realistically estimate the efforts required for the jobs and ensure they are equal or that the size difference between them is clear.

If a task has not been completed at the end of a sprint or a job is continuously shown as "ongoing" in a Kanban project, we have likely made a mistake in our estimation that should be corrected, the task should be broken down into more manageable parts, and our commitments should often be revised. Flexible management will ensure that the estimate focuses on the functions providing the highest value or that we need to tackle most quickly. However, the estimation itself is still relevant.

4. Know and control Limitations

Agile methodologies have limitations, and they must be taken into consideration. There are scope, deadline, cost, and quality factors that need to be met. Priorities might indeed be inverted, or the scope might be more negotiable, but the limitations on deadline, cost, and quality remain and must be managed.

These methods state that tasks should not exceed an absolute effort, define a maximum Work in Progress (WIP) we can manage or establish a time-box by using *sprints*. Limitations must be strictly maintained and not changed lightly, as they are an essential part of their model. If we make changes or adjustments and accept all types of changes, we are losing control.

5. Manage tension

Although it might seem contradictory, agile methodologies are more like a long-distance race than a sprint. Some organizations approach these methods as a way of moving more quickly – getting more done in less time – taking advantage of the fact that teams are more deeply involved. This is true, but if we want the implementation of these methods to last, we must manage team tension.

Having a motivated, results-focused, self-managed, and efficient team is possible with agile methodology. For these characteristics to last over time, we need to ensure that the team also perceives an improvement to productivity and not only a constant increase in effort and workload.

6. Metrics: "Power without control is useless."

These methods are compelling. They are capable of producing motivated teams that obtain impressive results in genuinely short spaces of time. Nonetheless, all this power does not come at odds with control. Agile methodologies encourage us to measure, analyze, and continuously improve.

Metrics are the way to explicit project management based on real data rather than intuition, opinions, or occasional emergencies. Speed, flow, and commitment compliance are all key metrics that we should gather and analyze to streamline our processes and improve our teams.

7. Quality

Quality means repeat business. Increasing delivery speeds, managing estimates incrementally, or having a self-managed team does not mean setting quality aside. It is imperative to deliver products quickly in agile methodologies, but those products should also work; they need to do what is required of them efficiently.

That is why it's important not to leave quality until the end and incorporate aspects of quality validation, revision, and measurement of all the items, deliverables and products we generate during the project from the outset.

8. Remain to the methodology rigorously

Agile methodologies have few rules, standards, or products. It is essential to follow the method precisely, especially at the start. It is better to change nothing (or almost nothing) before gaining experience. If something seems strange, have a little patience and give it a chance.

Scrum methods establish a series of roles, meetings, and stages that should be preserved, experienced, and maintained for these methods to work as we expect indeed. It is possible to go from less to more in these methods but follow their instructions precisely until you are comfortable with their use.

9. Revise and adjust the method

As soon as we have advanced significantly in the use of agile methodologies, we can consider making adjustments to them.

It is essential to conduct reviews or retrospective exercises that allow you to see what does and doesn't work within your organization and make the necessary changes to adapt the method to your culture style and requirements. However, this should always be done after having tried the standard models.

Agile methodologies are indeed flexible, very flexible, and that is why they can be adapted to almost any type of project, organization, or team. With a little experience, possible imbalances can be identified and changes, adaptations or additions can be made to these methods to ensure they perfectly suit our needs and circumstances.

10. Maximize visibility

One of the most important keys to the success of agile methodologies is visibility. Implementing these methods is done "behind the scenes" at some organizations, almost invisibly or as if applying this type of tool were embarrassing in some way.

It is vital for this type of implementation to be made visible, open and public so that the entire organization can see what is being done, how it is being done and what has been achieved by doing it.

Avoid using private "Kanban" methods or hiding them when the project client or sponsor appears. Be brave and show, explain, and harness the most obvious advantages. There is no better ally than a project client or sponsor that is involved in management, added to which agile methodologies enable maximum visibility and maximum participation from all stakeholders. An agile methodology is not an exception or an extravagance from an isolated team but something that can be applied throughout the organization.

11. Manage expectations

Many teams and organizations that embark down this path believe that all their problems will be solved as if by magic, that the client will never change their mind, that products will no longer have defects or that nothing "unpleasant" will ever happen during the project again.

Agile methodologies adapt very well to changing and stressful environments, but they are not the solution to every problem. Managing expectations from teams, clients, and management is essential to successful implementation.

The method may well not be perfect the first time around, that teams will feel uncomfortable with certain aspects of the processor that the project will encounter specific problems. This is completely normal. You will quickly see that progress is being achieved, that progress is significant, and that the results are very positive.

12. Select the right tools

Using a support tool when applying agile methodologies facilitates their implementation at organizations. Having centralized support for sharing information, measuring progress, and maintaining project control is highly essential. With the right tool, teams will be able to work independently while the organization can maintain control over project progress, costs, and revenue, efforts.

Do not be fooled by tools that are free but wholly disconnected from the rest of your organization. Agile methodologies are not an anecdotal or exceptional process implemented by teams with highly unprofessional tools; it is an important decision by the organization to adapt and improve. We are facing a project management revolution that is allowing us – with the right tools – to improve our performance, deliver high-value products very quickly, and achieve great success.

KEY METRICS TO MEASURE AGILE SUCCESS

Choosing the right agile metric to measure rapid success is simple, right? I wish that were the case, but in reality, selecting the correct agile metric can be a little tricky.

So, how do you get the most out of your agile metrics? The 9th annual State of Agile survey was reviewed, which compiles insights from nearly 4,000 respondents to find out how agile practitioners measure the success of their agile initiatives.

1. On-Time Delivery

According to the State of Agile survey, 58% of the respondents* said they measured the success of their agile efforts by on-time delivery.

With agile, our schedule is fixed, and our scope is flexed. What does that mean for on-time? Well, time happens, so theoretically, we are always on time. But, on-time is generally measured in context with the expectations about what will be delivered. To measure and have visibility of what is achieved, we may look to the out-of-the-box metrics of the burndown or the burnup.

2. Product Quality

A total of 48% of the respondents to the survey said they measured the success of their agile initiatives through product quality.

Quality is often measured in multiple ways, including looking at customer satisfaction, revenue growth, and the technical aspects of testing conducted throughout the development life cycle. With agile software development teams, we'll look at our velocity of completing working software with quality built-in. We tightly couple continuous testing and inspection throughout the lifecycle of the development, so we'll continuously be monitoring testing trends as well as continually inspecting build and code health.

For instance, in this testing trend chart, you can see the cumulative progress around testing activities. Ultimately you want to see all green, but a large amount of red along the line might reflect some issues in the codebase or process.

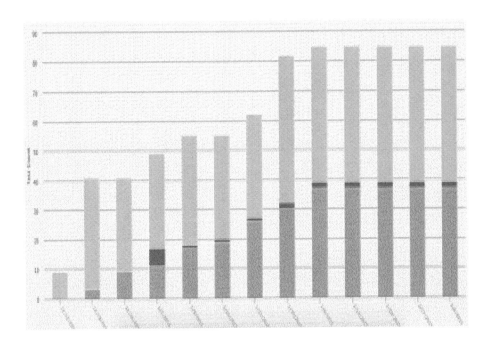

3. Customer/User Satisfaction

The survey found that 44% of respondents measured the success of their agile initiatives by customer or user satisfaction.

As with all these benefits, there are multiple ways to measure the outcomes. In the case of customer/user satisfaction, these include looking at the Net Promoter score, sales figures, several support calls vs. several features delivered in a period, or usage statistics of product or site capabilities.

4. Business Value

Approximately 44% of the respondents to the State of Agile survey stated that they measured the success of their agile initiatives by business value.

And several of the principles of the Agile Manifesto recognize the importance of delivering business value. Measuring business value is very explicit when we know that there's a contract for work to complete or a compliance need and fines if we don't finish the task. On the other hand, sometimes measuring value is prospective or speculative in the sense that the market inputs drive decisions, and the cost is often the best guess. Having a business value score applied to the features to be delivered can measure value.

Here's a sample epic cumulative flow chart based on value. The image helps you see the delivery of anticipated business value as features and other significant stories are complete.

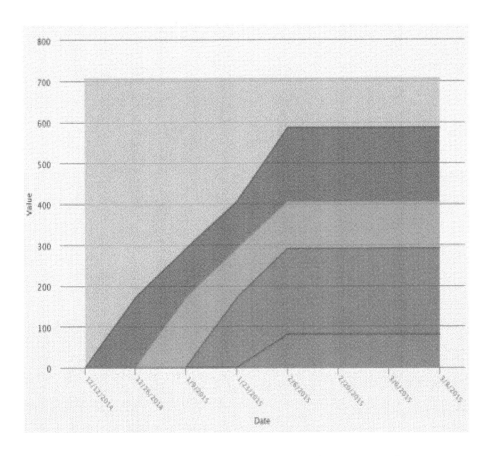

5. Product Scope (Features, Requirements)

Another 39% of the respondents answered that they measured the success of their agile initiatives with product scope.

Setting a goal around what to get done over the next three months, then tracking status, and getting it completed is hugely rewarding. Having real-time feedback as to the progress of work is valuable to everyone on the team, from the engineers to the program managers. With agile software development projects, you can always rely on the burndown charts, or visualize the progress of the cards moving from left-to-right on the project kanban board.

6. Project Visibility

Project visibility was the measure of choice for 30% of respondents to the survey.

One of the best ways to build trust is transparency. That means having the plans out in the open and making progress visible to all. Sharing progress at multiple dimensions provides the different stakeholders with information that makes sense from their point of view. Metrics that show features or overall progress against a targeted plan can provide great insights.

The other reason visibility is essential is because we need to have alignment among internal teams so they can best manage their work concerning component or service dependencies.

Understanding the impact of one team's work on another team is critical. By looking at the dependency chart below, it's easy to identify the stories at risk.

7. Productivity

According to the State of Agile survey, 29% of the respondents said they measured the success of their agile initiatives through productivity.

The concept of productivity in an agile world is a measure of outcomes, not output. So looking at burnup for a product or based on value is hugely impactful. Merely looking at a burnup of the count of stories or features over time is a great way to understand how much the team is delivering.

8. Predictability

Approximately 25% of the respondents from the survey said they measured the success of their agile initiatives by predictability.

A predominant metric used to assess predictability is the velocity trend. For a three- to four-month period, this shows how much work is at a sustainable pace on average. A velocity that wildly fluctuates might reflect a team that is changing, unpredictable work, or only a team that is still getting used to defining work small enough to complete in an iteration.

A velocity trend chart like the one below not only helps you see the performance but also gives you visibility into whether or not the team's output is at a predictable state – as this one shows.

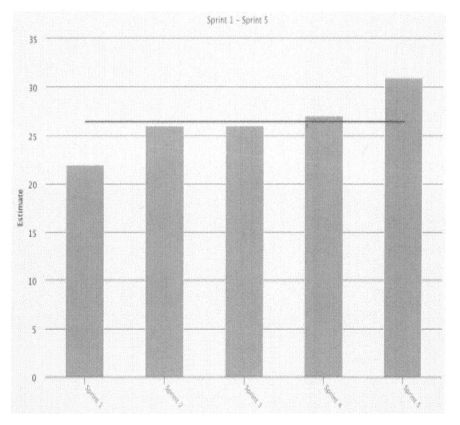

You can always try to assess velocity based merely on the count of story cards completed every week. This is usually the best indicator of predictability.

9. Process Improvement

Another 23% of the respondents said they measured the success of their agile initiatives by process improvement.

A core tenet of all lean and agile mindsets is continuous improvement – continually getting better. But how do you know you are getting better unless you measure the outcomes? There are all the metrics above that help, but there's also the constructive cumulative flow chart, which shows how well work is flowing through the lifecycle.

With this team level cumulative flow chart, you can see where bottlenecks or slowdowns may exist.

Also, there's cycle time – which helps us with planning and predictability. Cycle time is a great metric to view over time to see if process tweaks and adjustments are having an impact on productivity.

For instance, in this cycle time report, you can see the level of variability and performance across the various estimated pieces of work.

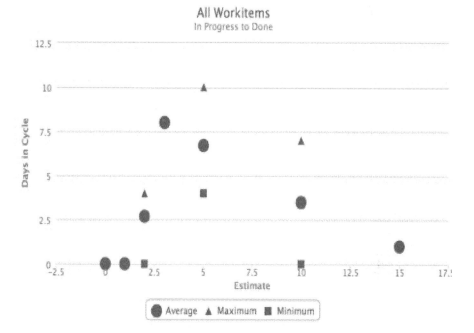

10. Don't Know

Just 11% of the State of Agile survey respondents said they didn't know! Well, if you don't know the benefits, try to start looking at the metrics above. You'll see improvements in delivered value, better quality around what produces, a more predictable cadence, and ultimately happier customers.

CONCLUSION

The Agile approach is often mistakenly considered to be a single methodology. Regardless of the exact methodologies and techniques they use, Agile teams have proven to increase profits 37 percent faster and generate 30 percent more revenue than non-agile companies. Higher speed, flexibility, and productivity achieved through such approaches are the key drivers that motivate more and more organizations to switch to Agile.

Software engineering, being an extremely fast-paced industry, calls for flexibility and responsiveness in every aspect of project development. Agile methodologies allow for delivering cutting-edge products and cultivating innovative experiences while keeping the product in sync with the market trends and user requirements.

However, there is always a place for diversity. Depending on your business requirements and goals, you might still benefit from using the Waterfall model or the combination of the two.

The Agile Method of software development does not guarantee success. Problems can still arise in the development process. Communication among team members can be faulty. Technology tools can fail. Customers can end up being unsatisfied with products.

It's also important to remember that with Agile, it's not a one-size-fits-all proposition. Different organizations have unique needs and challenges, both internally and externally. What works well for one enterprise might not work well for another.

But the potential benefits of Agile would seem to make the method worth considering for any company that produces software. As noted in a report on the Agile market by Transparency Market Research, "considering the rapid technological development taking place, businesses today need to be dynamic, be able to achieve faster-time-to market and at the same time reduce costs. Technology is a critical factor in which the success of a business depends. This calls for IT to be innovative, reliable, and adapt to changing requirements."

Agile development "promotes a disciplined approach to processes and involves checks and adaptations at various stages of software development," the report says. "This calls for accountability and results in encouraging the use of best engineering practices, resulting in the rapid delivery of quality software and business approaches aligned with customer needs."

With the proliferation of technology, devices, and applications, the services behind them have great importance, Transparency Market says, resulting in the IT industry needs to manage the services it provides increasingly. This, combined with the requirement to deliver more value, is likely to drive the growth of Agile development services.

As more organizations move toward digital transformation and attempt to enhance their data management capabilities, Agile will likely play an even more prominent role. A report by consulting firm McKinsey & Company, "Using Agile to Accelerate Your Data Transformation," notes that an Agile approach to data migration and management conveys some essential benefits, not the least of which is to declutter the business-information landscape.

"Data from multiple databases, functions, and business units can be combined and accessed more easily," the report says. "Companies can realize immediate value from the frequent release of minimally viable data-management solutions. Through the data mining made possible by the development of a comprehensive data lake, companies can also identify new business opportunities. And if business units are involved in data migration from the outset, they can seize these emerging opportunities more quickly or otherwise help the IT organization prioritize data- and digital transformation initiatives."

Agile is no longer just a methodology for software development or operations management; the firm says: "It is becoming a critical capability for those companies that want to manage their data more strategically and deliver seamless multichannel customer experiences.

Technology and business leaders would be wise to familiarize themselves with the Agile Method if they haven't already. For many organizations, it represents the way the work is in the age of digital transformation.